The New You

How to maximize your total appearance

BY

WILHELMINA

Illustrated by MANING

SIMON AND SCHUSTER/NEW YORK

Designed by Eve Metz
Manufactured in the United States of America

   2 3 4 5 6 7 8 9 10

Library of Congress Cataloging in Publication Data

Wilhelmina.
   The new you.
   I. Beauty, Personal.   I. Title.
RA778.W54   646.7′2   77-14188
ISBN 0-671-22487-5

I am most grateful for the generous help given by many individuals and corporations, including Sanford Buchsbaum of Revlon, Inc.; Barbara Buffa of *Brigitte* magazine; William Rayner of Condé Nast Publications Inc.; Franco Sartori of Edizioni Condé Nast, Italy; *L'Officiel de la Couture et de la Mode de Paris*; and Joan Streit of Germaine Monteil Cosmétiques.

For photographs used (pages 12 through 31)
Copyright © 1961, 1962, 1963, 1964, 1965, 1966 by the Condé
Nast Publications Inc.

And to such great photographers and friends whom I've had the pleasure of working with: David Cox, F. C. Gundlach, Horst, George Kufrin, Philip Pegler, Irving Penn, Victor Skrebneski, Bert Stern, Carl Turk and Curtis Williams.

My special thanks to Gary Bernstein.
To Mary Feeney, my assistant.
To Eve Metz and Delfina Rattazzi at Simon and Schuster.
And to all others who helped in any way.

CONTENTS

To Bruce, my husband,
without whom this book
might never have been written

INTRODUCTON

The first time I recall wishing for anything was when I stood behind the counter of my father's butcher shop in Culemborg, Holland. I was about four years old. To me, Father was the most beautiful man in the world as he went about his work in his starched white coat, greeting customers with a smile, filling their orders with pride. I longed to grow up to be the best butcher in the world; to be just like him. But he lost his dedicated apprentice a year or two later when I went to my first movie and discovered Jane living in the most exciting tree house imaginable. Surrounded by her own pet elephants and chimpanzee, she was loved by Tarzan, who made certain that crocodiles kept a respectful distance while she swam. Such fantasies filled my life for the next five years. At the advanced age of eleven, I had already dedicated my life, in an ever-changing pattern, to nursing, teaching and the glamorous but dangerous life of an international counterspy. Then, quite unexpectedly, came my Poppa's proudest moment. We were sitting at dinner when he delivered his proclamation: "Momma, Willy, today my application for entry into the United States has been approved. Tomorrow we begin to sell everything we own. We leave for Chicago in two months."

I slept very little that night, not knowing whether I cried more at the thought of leaving a lifetime of friends or from joy at the prospect of going to the land of golden opportunity.

It's strange to remember that we didn't even consider the fact that not one of us could speak or understand a single word of English. There were no Dutch-language courses in the Chicago high school I entered, so I did all my lessons by translating first from Dutch to German and then to English. That helped immensely, as did the television set in front of which I was glued evenings and weekends.

Soon I dreamed a new dream; one that stayed with me into adult life—a dream stimulated by my first exposure to American fashion magazines.

Quickly they became my favorite English reading material. I even went to secondhand stores to buy all the old issues I could afford on my rather meager allowance. As I grew up, I read them from cover to cover, devouring every word of the text and every picture of my new idols, the beautiful models who reached so glamorously from the pages—out to *me*.

Of course, I had no idea how one went about becoming a beautiful model. Before me lay a mysterious world replete with thousands of unanswered questions.

Then one day, a friend asked me to go with her to a local modeling school for an interview. She was frightened and needed my moral support. As it worked out, my friend was too short for a modeling career, but the director of the school assured me that I was exactly right. My head began to spin as I realized that perhaps my own life could prove to be an American dream transformed into a reality.

Poor Poppa. Morning, noon and night I plagued him. I pleaded. I begged him to help me make my dream come true. Finally he realized how much it meant to me and consented to my entering the school for an intensive course, on the condition that I repay the tuition. I was the happiest eighteen-year-old in Chicago. Tomorrow my world was to open.

And open it did. For the next nine years, in Chicago, in Paris and finally in New York, I lived out my dream and fulfilled my most cherished fantasies. If I had it all to do over again, would I change anything? What did I learn from my experiences and personal observations during those years that I might share with others?

Only ten years ago I was a working model. Today, I am the key executive of one of the largest model agencies in the world. Perhaps I am one of very few people fortunate enough to have stood on both sides of the beauty-business fence in such a short span of time. I can only hope that some of the things I learned the hard way will provide inspiration for other girls and women who wish for a life of exciting attractiveness and good health. I have written this book for every woman interested in finding her own "look"—the look that professional models work so hard to acquire and maintain.

Real beauty begins with the food you eat. The choice affects your hair, skin, teeth and nails as well as the proportions of your figure. There is no substitute for the glow of health that comes from proper diet.

Women of all ages who grace the pages of fashion magazines, those who appear in national advertising, those who are familiar to us on our television and movie screens have the same figure, clothing and cosmetic problems to consider as women who assume other roles in our society. There are only a

Introduction

few perfect natural beauties in the world who need not resort to the cosmetic and other aids available to us today. Women who want to project an aura of beauty must give time and thought to their appearance just as models do. A model's highest hurdle is maintaining proper weight for presentations before the camera. Women in all walks of life face the same challenge.

Catering to the model's primary concern is the advice in Chapter 3 of this book on sensible eating. Sensible means confining oneself to only one medium-sized portion of a tasty food, avoiding fried or creamy foods that often have an undesirable effect on weight and on complexion. Of course, rich, luscious desserts are taboo. Most doctors, dietitians and nutritionists recommend a single serving of a simple dessert as the conclusion of the meal. So I have offered a variety of gastronomic delights that are unelaborate but satisfying and eye-appealing. Dessert should never be the villain in a beautiful woman's fight against avoirdupois.

What you *do* eat is as important as what you avoid. Good nutrition is the keynote. These recipes are the basis for achieving a proper balance of all kinds of nutritious foods.

I have designed my "Hummingbird Diet" for women who, like models, wish to overcome even the slightest gain in weight. There are times when we all fall prey to dinner-party dining. When the hostess' specialties are too appetizing to resist, there is nothing wrong with an occasional food binge. But afterward, profit from "the model's secret strategy": for a day or two stick to one of these fast-loss routines, so that your clothes won't feel two sizes too small. That's what I do.

Models are interested in overall beauty as well as figure control, and I have devoted several chapters to revelations of techniques we use to achieve sparkling attractiveness.

For example: Models know that exercise tones up the figure. We know we have to consider the special contours of our bodies when selecting a proper wardrobe. We know that our hair, skin, hands and feet must be at their best at all times, and so I am going to pass our hints along to all women who admire the "model's look."

Recipes, nutritional information, an exercise program, beauty and fashion hints—I have gathered them all together in this volume. With them I hope to set the pace for the modern woman who is determined to step into the world with the confidence and sense of well-being that come from an outer appearance of good grooming and an inner feeling of health and beauty, in every activity of her life—day and night.

At the age of four with my brother Walter in Utrecht, Holland.
The year is 1943 and I'm the one on the right.

Nine years old and living in Oldenburg, Germany.

At the Blumenhof Grammar School in Oldenburg.

With my dog, Axel, in front of my family's butcher shop. I was thirteen years old.

My 1958 graduation picture from Waller High School in Chicago.

With Ron Tuhy, my Senior Prom escort.

I brought my grandmother to Chicago from Germany in 1960 to cele brate her seventy-fifth birthday. Here we all are: Father, Grandma Mother and Uncle Fritz.

Test shots taken in Chicago for my very first promo- tional material, a "glossy." I had changed my name to Winnie Hart at that time.

Another
school picture.

A test shot taken while working
toward my first composite
in Chicago.
Photo/George Kufrin

High-school pictures taken for the Homecoming Queen contest. I did not win that contest, nor did I win the Most Likely to Succeed contest. I was in modeling school at the time.

Back-and-available card, which I had made when I returned to Chicago after my first trip to Paris.

These passport photographs were taken for my trip to Paris.

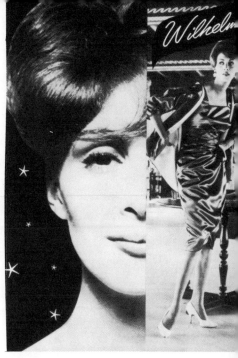

Wilhelmina

MEASUREMENTS	
Size	10 & 12
Height S/F	5'9"
Bust	35
Waist	23
Hips	35
Hair	Med. Brown
Eyes	Brown
Shoe	8½ AA
Glove	7½
Hat	22

PATRICIA STEVENS, INC.
22 West Madison Street
Chicago, Illinois
State 2-9107

My first model's composite. The true beginning of a glamorous and rewarding career. I am now Wilhelmina and no longer Winnie Hart.

Photos/Skrebneski, George Kufrin, Dick Boyer and Jim Crotzer

Another back-and-available card taken just before I moved to New York.

New York. Out for dinner at the Latin Quarter in 1965. Skinny me with my husband, Bruce, and Sherri, Bruce's eldest daughter.

Sharing my first successes with my parents. They were now finally convinced that I was going to make it as a model.

Photo/Carl Turk

4

ECTIONS
E HAUTE
OUTURE
PARIS

My one and only
New York com-
posite, printed in
1966.

WILHELMINA

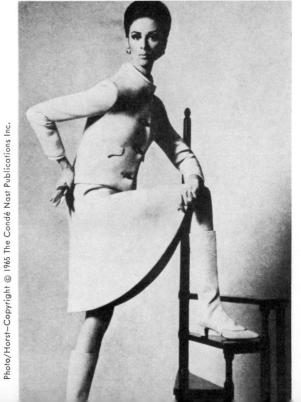

After three or four months in Paris, I did my first international cover—for *L'Officiel*. It was shot in the Sahara.

Photo/Roland de Vassal—© Editions Condé Nast, France

This is my first Vic Skrebneski photograph, for which he scrubbed my face and personally did my hair and make-up. He helped me develop an entirely new image.

Photo/Skrebneski

Another Skrebneski test shot, done in Chicago in 1961.

Photo/Skrebneski

A picture taken for one of my steady fur accounts, which brought me to Hamburg twice a year. It's an ocelot coat. I always thought my profile left something to be desired, but I ended up doing a lot of profile shots in my time.
Photo/F. C. Gundlach

Revlon lights up your night life with a dazzling new make-up!
(So flattering you'll never again wear ordinary make-up after dark)

'frosted touch & glow'... shimmers softly like a
million tiny stars. There's liquid make-up to illuminate your face with a
subtly-frosted glow. Frosted face powder adds a translucent pearl-
and-diamond finish. And the frosted pressed powder creates
instant radiance. If history is made at night, this is where you begin!

new evening make-up collection by Revlon

Photo/F. C. Gundlach

I think people thought of me mostly for makeup, hats and furs. The pictures
below were taken in Lapland.

PELZE
IN DER
MITTERNACHTS-
SONNE

Oben: Der Jähre-Fjord, ein
norwegischer Schlitten und ein
Mantel aus SAGA-Nerzen.

Mitte: In die Kulisse des Varanger-Fjordes
gestellt: Ein Paletot aus SAGA-Pearl-Nerzen,
mit und ohne Gürtel zu tragen.

Links: Vor den typischen
bunten Fischerhäusern
in Kirkenes: Ein Mantel
aus SAGA-Silverblue-Nerzen.

Rechts: Im Lager nomadisierendes
Lappen: Der Mantel aus Somali-Leopard,
tragbar mit und ohne Gürtel

Photo/F. C. Gundlach

24

NOVITA'

ottobre 1964 n. 163

IN ESCLUSIVA
AUDREY
HEPBURN
PRESENTA:
GLI ABITI
DI GIVENCHY
I COSTUMI
DI MY
FAIR LADY

I was lucky to work a lot with
the great Penn. On the right
is one of my favorite pictures
out of my model book.

25

My last *Vogue* cover, photographed by Penn for the Christmas issue, my head inside a solid-gold bird cage studded with diamonds.

I quickly learned patience and endurance in uncomfortable situations. I had to cancel the next day's booking after the photograph on the right, because the branches had so badly scratched my neck.

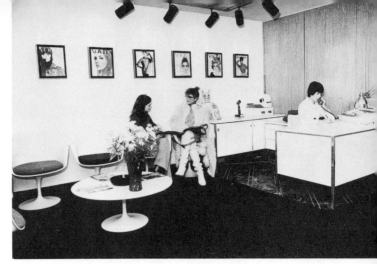

1

2

3

4

An insight into Wilhelmina Models, Inc., of which I am president. It has been in existence since 1967.

1—As an instructor to my new girls in our photo studio, which doubles as a classroom.
2—The reception area.
3—The men's booking room.
4—The women's booking room.
5—Counseling one of my girls, Ginny Pauley, in my office.
6—Bruce and I checking a contact sheet of one of our new discoveries, Will Russell.

Photos/David Cox

29

6

Wedding portrait, 1966. I met Bruce during my first appearance on the "Johnny Carson Show," where he was working as a production executive.
Photo/Philip Pegler

Here I am eight and a half months pregnant with Jason, in 1974.
Photo/Gary Bernstein

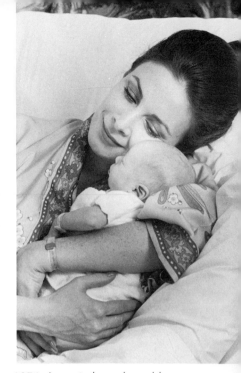

Our daughter, Melissa, when four months old, in 1968. This was a Germaine Monteil ad for a Christmas package.

Photo/Courtesy of Germaine Monteil Cosmétiques

1974. Jason is three days old.

Photo/Curtis Williams

Family portrait taken during the summer of 1975.

Photo/Gary Bernstein

31

CHAPTER 1

Taking a Look at Yourself

My world, the world of the professional model, is probably the most overglamorized, most inadvertently misrepresented, of all professions. During the past decade, models have been publicized and worshiped as never before; at the same time, they have been deprecated as beautiful idiots and narcissistic statues devoid of feeling for anyone but themselves. We, in the profession, must take a large share of the blame: the fashion press too often caters to the public demand for stories about personalities who live in a whipped-cream dream world filled to the brim with possibilities for fame, fortune and excitement. The public conception of a modeling career has been distorted beyond reality.

Models are as vulnerable as the rest of humanity. Every trait, both good and bad, can be found in the model's character. But one of the big differences between a model and any other pretty girl is that a model understands her own face and figure and knows how to make the best of them. It's something on which she has focused all her energies in the same way that any working woman tackles her job. It started the first moment she took a long, truthful look at herself and made an analysis of her attributes and her defects. It's the sort of self-examination any beauty must go through to study ways in which she can learn to play up her good points and play down or eliminate the bad.

I am convinced that all successful models—all beautiful women, for that matter—have one single thing in common. It isn't a perfect nose, a flawless skin, a refined bone structure; it is simply that they *care:* enough so that *through constant effort* they make the most of what was given them at birth. I know, because my decision to become a model forced me to recognize my own imperfections. I made a list. My head is actually too small for my body; my hair too fine, and there isn't enough of it; my profile leaves much to be desired and I wage constant battles to control my weight and keep my skin unblemished. Yet given all these seemingly hopeless liabilities, I managed to turn them into assets, because I cared; and I still care! By trial and error I learned—and I am still learning.

All you need for your personal beauty evaluation is an hour or so of your time, a measuring tape, a full-length mirror—and of course, the sincere intention of being completely honest with yourself.

POSTURE CHECK

Start with a posture check. Models are known for their graceful, relaxed posture. That means standing with head high, but level—not looking up into space. Your shoulders should be comfortably back, and your chest should be held high. Stomach should be flat, and buttocks should be tucked in and under. Stand with your knees slightly relaxed, not rigid, and with your feet pointed straight ahead, heels about two to three inches apart.

To check your posture from the side, hang a string down the center of a full-length mirror. Stand sideways and have someone check for you. Your ears, shoulders and body should follow the straight line of the string. If your ears aren't in line with your shoulders, if your shoulders slump forward or if your torso obviously sways to the front or back of the string, your posture needs work.

Check your sitting posture too. Good sitting posture means sitting tall in the chair with your spine straight, but again, not rigid. Sit back in the chair on your pelvic bones, not your spine or waistline. Rest your back (not head or shoulders) against the back of the chair. This posture not only looks better, but helps avert back trouble.

BODY CHECK

One simple body check is the pinch test. Measuring tape aside, it can tell you if your body needs shaping, firming up or trimming down. Check the strategic body spots—places where flab is bound to show up if you're out of shape. They are the back of your upper arm, the midriff and just below your shoulder blade. Pinch with your thumb and forefinger; if you have more than an inch of flesh in your pinch, you have an excess of fat.

For most girls, a scale is a pretty good test of excessive fat too. Some people, such as sports stars or construction workers, may be over their normal weight without having fatty tissue—their mass is solid muscle; but when women are overweight, they're usually flabby too. To check your weight, step on a good, accurate scale; then compare your results with the Desirable Weight Chart on page 36. It shows your healthy weight range in ratio to your body proportions. Choose the weight within the range that is most suitable to your structure. Models generally aim for the lowest healthy weight, since they have to be bone-slim to photograph well.

For more specific body analysis, strip down to your panties and bra and start measuring from the top down. Be honest—don't pull the measuring tape too tight. Measure your bust, waist and hips and compare them with the Desirable Proportions Chart on page 36. If your proportions need work, don't be discouraged—there's hardly a model who started out perfect. It takes work. Fill in those measurements in the "Comments" column of the Beauty Report List on page 39. Do the same with the following measurements: upper arm; thigh; calf (at the thickest point) and ankle (at the thinnest point). Take your measurements and mark them weekly. You can watch your progress as you exercise, and diet if you need it.

BEAUTY CHECK

The next part of your self-analysis deals with your general appearance. Start from the top here too. What about your hair? Do you always keep it swingy-clean and shiny? Does it need a trim—or maybe even restyling? Could your color stand a little revving up? Decide what, if anything, needs work and mark it down in the "Comments" column of the Beauty Report List.

DESIRABLE WEIGHT CHART

HEIGHT* (shoes on)	SMALL FRAME	MEDIUM FRAME	LARGE FRAME
4'10"	92–98	96–107	104–119
4'11"	94–101	98–110	106–122
5'0"	96–104	101–113	109–125
5'1"	99–107	104–116	112–128
5'2"	102–110	107–119	115–131
5'3"	105–113	110–122	118–134
5'4"	108–116	113–126	121–138
5'5"	111–119	116–130	125–142
5'6"	114–123	120–135	129–146
5'7"	118–127	124–139	133–150
5'8"	122–131	128–143	137–154
5'9"	126–135	132–147	141–158
5'10"	130–140	136–151	145–163
5'11"	134–144	140–155	149–168
6'0"	138–148	144–159	153–173

Women ages 25 and over†

*Calculated for height in 2" heels, so add 2" to your stocking-feet height.

†For girls between 18 and 25, subtract 1 pound for each year under 25. For girls planning a modeling career, subtract 8 to 10 pounds.

DESIRABLE PROPORTIONS CHART

Height 4'10"–5'
Bust: 30–31
Waist: 19–20
Hips: 31–32

Height 5'1"–5'4"
Bust: 32–33
Waist: 20–21
Hips: 33–34

Height 5'5"–5'7"
Bust: 33–34
Waist: 21–23
Hips: 33–34

Height 5'8"–5'9"
Bust: 34–35
Waist: 23–24
Hips: 34–35

Height 5'10"–6'
Bust: 35–37
Waist: 25–26
Hips: 35–37

Taking a Look at Yourself

To check your face, sit comfortably at a well-lighted mirror. Is your complexion blotchy or bumpy? What about its tone—is it too sallow, pink or pale? Is the tone even? Are your pores small, or do they need shrinking? If your skin is oily, are you handling it properly? Dry and combination skins have special problems too. Are you giving your skin all the care it needs?

Have you ever been ruthless in looking at your facial problems? Do your eyes seem too small, your nose too long or your mouth too full? If you can analyze your face the way you analyze your body, you'll be better able to find the hair and makeup styles that look best on you. Mark down any problems you have and learn how to compensate for them.

Good looks don't stop at your head; they take in your whole body. In fact, your hands are as important as your face—they are just as expressive. Do you keep your hands soft, well manicured? Are your nails in good condition and your cuticles smoothed? Are you meticulous about defuzzing legs and underarms, and keeping your elbows, knees and feet as soft as can be?

These things go into the making of all polished beauties. Handsome women don't just happen. They're created through the same kind of discipline it takes to do anything well, to be anything worthwhile.

The most elusive aspect of the modeling profession is finding your "look" and then seeking ways to merchandise that look properly. Most people think only in terms of changes in face and hair. Actually, that's only part of the picture; the total person is involved.

A classic example of all that I have told you here is the success story of one of our young models. I remember when she first entered my agency, only fourteen years old and fresh from Vestavia, Alabama. She was by no means the vibrant, professional, eye-catching fashion figure of a few short months later, but she had three things in her favor that made discovering her "look" a relatively simple matter: she had all the necessary physical attributes; she had a keen intelligence and she had a burning desire to succeed. Her appetite for work matched that of the most dedicated professional persons I have ever encountered.

We believed in each other. Together we decided to change her "look" from head to toe. We had no time to dally. Luckily for our project, she arrived in New York during summer vacation, so we didn't need to squeeze her make-over between classes. By the time school resumed in the fall, she was already well on her way.

We began by experimentation with a series of hairstyles, makeup applications, photo sessions. We reexamined our results. When we were displeased, we tried something else. True to tradition in our field, she was helped tremendously by the photographers for whom she worked during the early stages of her career. They offered professional suggestions as to modifications in makeup, hairstyle, posture and other qualities that could help her find her *distinctive* self. She became increasingly aware of fashion trends. She began to study line and color. She worked toward improving her taste in clothes. As her budget permitted, her wardrobe took on a whole new "style."

With these external changes came new mutations in her attitude and personality. It was as though a new person—a more confident one—had been born. As her weekly income moved upward, she realized that she was really making the grade in a difficult, competitive business. What followed was the real test of her intelligence: never once, not for a minute, was she ever self-satisfied. She continued to experiment with hairstyles and makeup techniques until she became so deft at transformation that she could create three different illusions for the client during one booking. This chameleon quality is extremely valuable to a photographer. It helps him exercise his own flexibility, so our model is continually rebooked. She is pleasant to work with, completely professional in her approach, considerate of others and talented. Who could ask for anything more?

Such discipline as this takes motivation. And nothing is quite so motivating as a list. Facts show up for what they are: they show what needs improvement, and they chart improvement along the way. That's what the Beauty Report List on the next two pages is for. Do use it to find your own "look."

BEAUTY REPORT LIST

	1st WEEK	2nd WEEK	3rd WEEK
Posture			
Weight			
Measurements			
Bust			
Waist			
Hips			
Upper arms			
Thighs			
Calves			
Ankles			
Hair			
Skin			
Face			
Body			
Makeup			
Grooming			

COMMENTS

(continued on next page)

BEAUTY REPORT LIST (continued)

	4th WEEK	5th WEEK	6th WEEK
Posture			
Weight			
Measurements			
Bust			
Waist			
Hips			
Upper arms			
Thighs			
Calves			
Ankles			
Hair			
Skin			
Face			
Body			
Makeup			
Grooming			

COMMENTS

BEAUTY PLAN

Now that you've worked up all the motivation you need, set down a beauty schedule for yourself. Looking great takes time, but with practice you can tailor your beauty routine to fit into the other activities of your life.

Be realistic about it: If you have a family to feed at six o'clock, don't plan to take your facial at five. If you like to sleep until the last possible second and that condition is incurable, leave the morning exercise stint to the morning people.

The fact that you're busy doesn't mean you ought not to take time for yourself. Many women with families or those with a lot of responsibility on the job feel guilty when they take a few minutes to attend to their own good looks. That's upside-down thinking. They not only owe the time to themselves; they owe it to their families and to their colleagues at work. Every woman can find time for beauty if she budgets her energies wisely—if she breaks down her schedule into the daily and weekly beauty tasks you see below.

DAILY BEAUTY TASKS

At least fifteen minutes of exercise
Face cleansing morning and night
Shower or bath
Makeup and touch-ups
Hair and touch-ups
Beauty relaxation

Other things can be done once a week or so. Some women prefer to keep one night a week free and do everything at once. Others devote just a few minutes before going to bed each night to one particular task, spreading out their beauty routine day by day. Both methods work. It's consistency of effort that leads to good grooming.

WEEKLY BEAUTY TASKS

Manicure
Pedicure
Defuzzing legs and underarms (twice a week for some)
Shampoo and set (more or less often, depending upon hair)
Tweeze eyebrows

Once you've established your beauty schedule, make up your mind to follow it faithfully. It may require self-discipline at first, but before you know it, it will be second nature. You'll have developed good habits that will stay with you and lead to a lifetime of beauty.

CHAPTER 2

Body-Shaping Exercises

Even though most models look inch-perfect, there's hardly one who started out that way or who stays that way without exercise. To look super, nearly all figures need concentrated work. Exercise is important in any meaningful beauty plan. To be really effective, it has to be more than occasional. It has to be constant. Exercise each day if you can. If you can't, don't give up; a three-times-a-week program is consistent too— as long as it's three times *every* week.

Whichever you choose, regular exercise will make you healthier, happier and mentally more alert. Simple acts of day-to-day living force us to exercise to some degree. Every morning, for example, we do at least one sit-up, since it's easier to slip out of bed from a sitting position than it would be if we stayed flat on our backs and rolled out. We do at least one waist exercise and one leg exercise as we grope around for our bedroom slippers and stand to meet the new day head on. And so it goes through the balance of each day: picking up a pencil that has dropped; climbing a few steps to reach the loge section of a movie house; lifting the telephone or moving the typewriter; drinking a glass of water—or any of the thousand other "accidental" exercises we do daily. This is nature's way of keeping us from being marshmallows. Having a really healthy body and mind takes added effort that is planned, programmed and performed with some degree of fidelity.

While I'm not by any stretch of the imagination a physical-education nut, neither am I a sports wallflower. My personal preferences are swimming, scuba diving and skiing—though I'm not very good at the last one; when I was modeling I always had to worry about the condition of my arms and legs. I even enjoy taking some very unprofessional swings at a tennis ball and confess that sports are more to my liking than regimented exercises.

43

I might as well be perfectly honest and admit that I don't enjoy deep knee bends, jumping rope and all the other in-place physical-fitness exercises as much as sports. However, when I have to do them, I try to psych myself into having fun. When I realize I'm getting a bit flabby here and there. I usually go into one of these two-to-three week demand-exercise programs. Once I force myself into a crash routine, sit-ups and all the rest of it become less objectionable with each succeeding day. By the fourth or fifth day I actually love the feeling of renewed mental and physical well-being. I should continue with regularity, but the truth is, I don't. As soon as I've accomplished my goal, I foolishly set it all aside; but the minute I hear my husband or one of our models remark, "Is that the beginning of a tummy I see?" I go back to my combination of exercise and diet. It works every time.

Experience has taught me that whether we wish to admit it or not, we pay a price for everything in life. When we're young, we pay the price of getting as good an education as we can. Or instead, we neglect our schooling and pay a far greater price later on because we did not take advantage of our opportunities. The same applies to physical fitness and figure control. Ill health can be costly. Don't miss the chance to stay in good condition. The price is not high: a little time and effort.

The amount of time you should exercise depends upon your physical condition. It's a good idea to get a checkup from your doctor before starting an exercise program. If nothing prevents you from exercising, he can estimate how much you can tackle and how quickly you can progress.

Once you know your limits, stay within them. If you try to double your exercise time, you may increase your appetite to giant proportions too, and gain weight instead of losing it, which is one of the objectives of the exercise.

Exercise won't, by the way, burn enough calories to cause any appreciable weight loss. Only cutting calories will do that. But on the theory that every calorie burned counts, exercise will help. Besides, by firming and toning you, exercise will help you to a better body—not just a smaller one.

When you exercise, wear the most comfortable thing you can find—a leotard, a knit swimsuit, pajamas or anything that moves easily. Don't wear anything binding—and certainly not a girdle. Find a comfortable place to exercise someplace with plenty of free space and a thick rug. If you don't have a cushioning rug, make your own exercise mat with towels and an inch-thick slab of foam rubber. Sew together three sides of the towels and slip in the foam-rubber slab (one inch narrower and two inches shorter than the towels). Sew snaps on the open end of the towel case to close it. Then the foam slab slips out easily so that you can launder the case.

On the next few pages are a variety of exercises—Warm-ups, Spot Shapers and Kitchen Exercises. Each time you exercise, start with the Warm-ups—do all of them. Then choose a few of the Spot Shapers. Don't try doing all of them at once. There are several exercises for some areas. Do one one time, another the next. Variety is more interesting and you're more likely to be faithful to your program that way. Squeeze in the Kitchen Exercises while you're waiting for water to boil or cookies to bake or whenever there's a fraction of a minute that might otherwise be wasted.

WARM UPS

STRETCH

Stand erect, feet slightly apart and arms at your sides. Then stand on tiptoe and stretch your arms up as though reaching—one hand first, then the other, finally both together. Then bend from your waist to touch the floor.

TORSO TWIST

Stand with feet about shoulder width apart, arms stretched straight out to your sides. Bend from your waist to reach your right foot with your right hand. Return to an upright position, then bend the same way to touch your left foot with your left hand.

CURL

Lie on a soft surface on your back. Pull your knees up to your chin and clasp your hands around your legs. Rock gently back and forth.

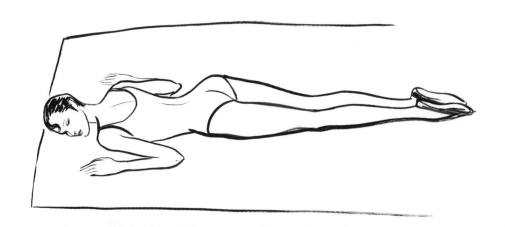

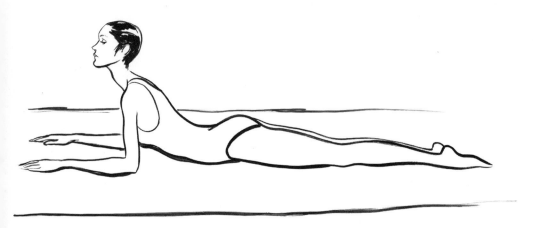

COBRA

Lie on your stomach, legs together, arms bent at the elbows and tucked close to your body. Slowly raise your head and shoulders until they are propped up on your elbows.

Then gradually straighten your arms and arch your back. Finally, bend your legs back with toes pointed.

SPOT SHAPERS

WAIST

Sit with your legs out straight, toes pointed and hands above your head.

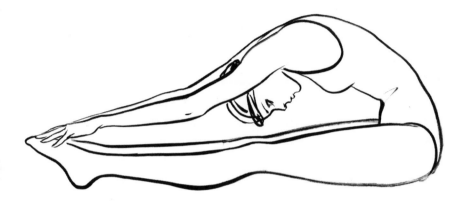

Bend forward from the waist and touch your toes with your hands. As you progress, touch your head to your knees.

WAIST

Stand with hands on hips. Lean to one side as far as you can, then to the front, other side and back. Don't move your hips as you make the circle. Do this for about one half to one minute.

WAIST AND LEGS

Stand with feet together, hands above your head. Keeping your legs straight at the knees, bend from your waist and touch your toes with the tips of your fingers.

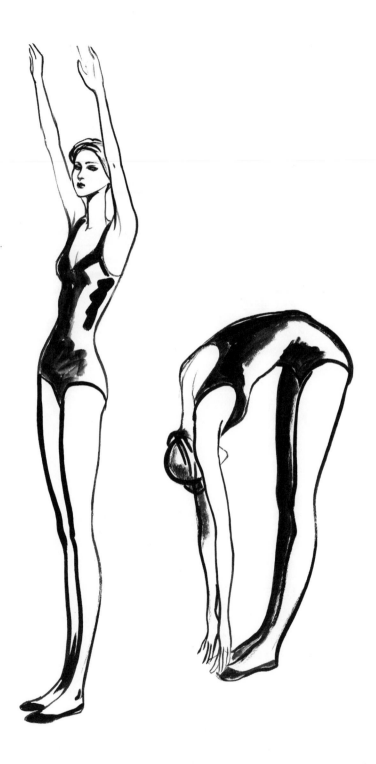

WAIST AND LEGS

Hold on to the back of a steady chair and move back until your arms are straight. Raise one foot to the back of the chair, straighten your leg and touch your head to your leg. Lower the leg and repeat with the other one.

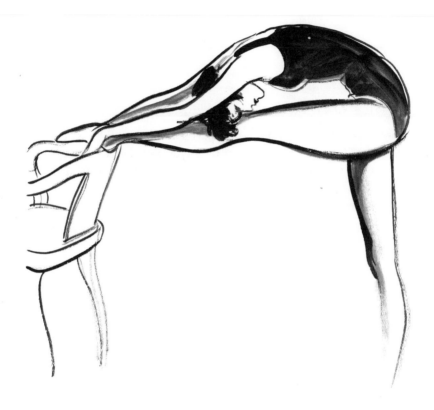

WAIST AND HIPS

Stand with feet about a half yard apart and clasp your hands behind your neck. From the waist, bend back as far as you can, then to the right. Repeat for the left side. Concentrate on keeping your elbows back as far as you can. Feel the stretch.

WAIST AND THIGHS

Lie face down. Bend your legs back and grasp them with your hands at the ankles. Keeping your back arched and head back as far as possible, rock back and forth like a rocking chair.

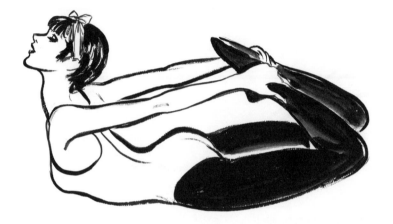

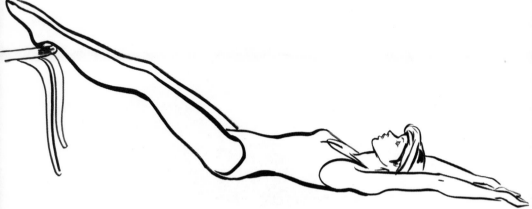

WAIST AND ABDOMEN

Lie on your back with arms stretched over your head and your legs propped up on a chair. Pull yourself up and touch your toes. Lie back and repeat—once or twice at first, but work up to five.

WAIST AND ABDOMEN

Sit straight with legs apart and arms back, supporting part of your body weight. Flex your stomach muscles to lift your legs off the floor a few inches. Hold for the count of ten.

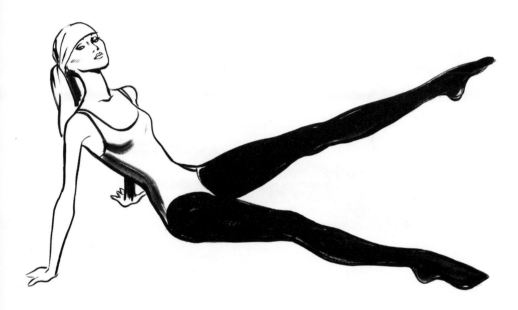

ABDOMEN AND THIGHS

Sit with legs apart and lean back on your arms. Raise both legs a few inches off the ground, move them in opposing circles five times, then reverse directions.

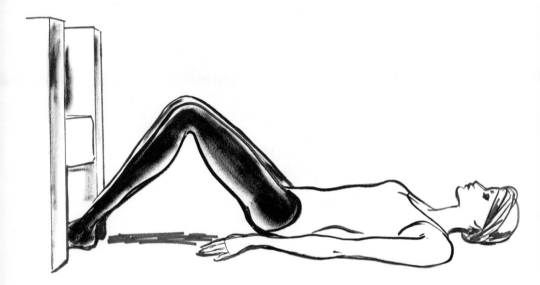

ABDOMEN AND THIGHS

Lie on the floor, arms at your side with ankles anchored under a sturdy chair. Using your stomach muscles and extending your arms for balance, lift your torso. Hold for a few seconds, lie back and repeat—once or twice at first, but work up.

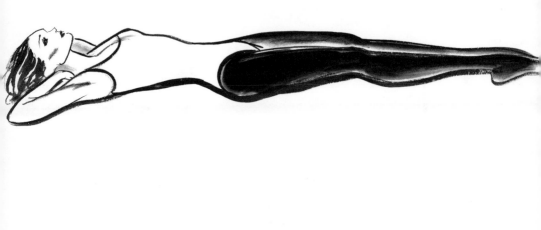

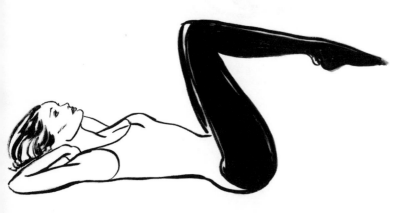

ABDOMEN

Lie on your back, hands behind your neck and legs straight and together. Bend your knees toward your chest; then slowly straighten your legs until they're at a 90-degree angle with your torso. With your legs straight, lower them together slowly to the floor.

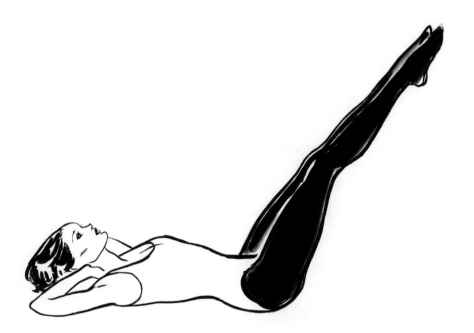

ABDOMEN AND LEGS

Lie with legs flexed, arms stretched above your head. Lift your hips from the floor and stretch your legs above your head, trying to touch the floor between your hands. Then roll on your spine to a sitting position with your knees bent and arms straight out. Lean forward on your feet and slowly rise to a standing position.

BUTTOCKS

Stand erect holding on to the back of a chair. Lift your right leg at the knee and bend your head and neck forward to meet it. Then kick that leg back as high as possible and arch your back. Do this four more times; then repeat with your left leg.

BUTTOCKS

Kneel on your hands and knees. Bend your right knee up to your chest; then slowly kick your leg back as high as you can and arch your back. Repeat four times; then repeat for left leg.

BUTTOCKS

Lie face down on the floor, your legs straight and arms stretched above your head. Tighten your shoulder, back and buttocks muscles enough to lift your arms and legs off the floor. Hold for the count of ten.

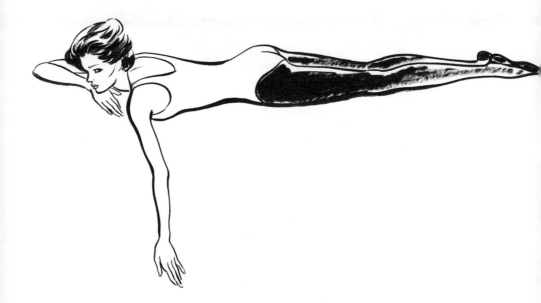

BUTTOCKS

Lie face down, your chin on your right hand, left arm stretched straight out. Raise your left leg and hold tightly with buttocks muscle for the count of five. Reverse hand positions and repeat for the right leg.

BUTTOCKS

Lie face down, your legs apart and hands folded under your face. Raise your legs a few inches from the ground keeping the rest of your body perfectly still. Move your legs in opposing circles five times; then reverse directions.

HIPS AND THIGHS

Stand straight, hands on your hips, and bend your right leg, bringing the foot up to your left knee. Slowly straighten your leg to the front; then bring it to the side of your body. Lower and repeat the same exercise for your left leg.

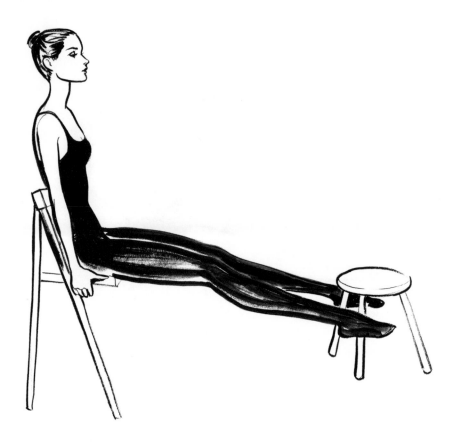

HIPS AND THIGHS

Sit straight on a chair with your legs extended to a stool. Pinch the outsides of the stool legs with the insides of your feet with maximum force; then put your feet inside the stool legs and try to push them out with maximum force.

HIPS AND LEGS

Lie on your right side, your right arm under your head, the left extended to the front and legs together. Lift and lower your left leg slowly five times. Concentrate on keeping it straight. Then turn to your left side and do the same for your right leg—again five times.

THIGHS AND CALVES

Stand erect with your feet together, arms straight out in front. Slowly bend at your knees (keeping your heels flat on the floor) until you feel a pull at

the front of your thighs. Then clasp your hands behind your neck, hold this position and count to five. Then extend your arms again and squat down, heels still flat on the floor. Keeping your back erect, stand straight again.

THIGHS AND CALVES

Get into an upside-down bicycling position. Lie on your back and leaning on your hands, lift your hips high off the ground. Move your legs as though riding a bicycle.

BUST

Stand with your arms outstretched, weighted with empty bottles, books or dumbbells in your hands. Swing the weights in a large circle keeping your arms straight, the rest of your body still. Circle forward, then backward, five times each.

BUST

Stand with your legs apart. Bend forward from your waist and clasp a rod, rolling pin or ruler in your hands behind your back. Pull the object in your hands up in back as far as you can. Really stretch.

BUST

Clench your fists at the sides of your waist and try to touch your elbows behind you. Hold for ten seconds. Then clasp your hands in front of you and push the palms together, contracting your arm and chest muscles.

CHIN FIRMER I

Any time—turn your head very very slowly, first in one direction, then in the other.

CHIN FIRMER II

Slowly tilt your head back as far as you can—as though you were looking to the sky. Then slowly tilt it forward until your chin nearly rests on your chest.

MUSCLE STRETCHER

Grab the back of a chair, bending your body from the waist and keeping your arms straight. Lower your head below arm level and relax. Remember to keep your legs straight.

DEEP BREATHING

One super exercise to practice in the kitchen or anywhere—anytime you think of it. It's an allover beauty exercise that benefits hair, skin and general health in two ways: it stirs up circulation and helps ease tension. Models find it particularly useful anytime they're in a rush and begin to feel tension mount. That's one reason it has a very special place in the kitchen. Here's how it works. 1) Inhale through your nose very slowly and deeply; slowly expand your stomach as you inhale. 2) Exhale slowy through your nose, emptying your lungs of as much air as you can; at the same time, slowly pull in your stomach as far as you can. Do this a few times and you can practically feel tension melting away.

BEHIND TUCK

Another anytime exercise—anytime you think of it, whether you're standing or sitting. Simply tighten your buttocks muscles as firm as you can, hold for five seconds and release. Do this a few times every day and you'll never have to cram for bikini season.

CHAPTER 3

The Hummingbird Diet: Eating for Beauty

I am the best weight loser in the world, and I have a long dieter's past to prove it.

When I arrived in New York from Paris, I was, without a doubt, the fattest model the town had ever welcomed. Paris has a way of sneaking up on a girl and it had done an excellent job on me. I shudder to remember that I weighed 149 pounds. So it was adieu to Maxim's and those superb crêpes suzette; and bon soir to the Left Bank bistros and the boeuf bourguignon with crusty bread fresh from the boulangeries that sopped up the broth; and farewell to L'Orangerie and the St.-Honoré, a pyramid of cream puffs and whipped cream held together by caramel. Today, I get vicarious appetite appeasement just remembering those gourmet delicacies.

I fooled the camera in Europe because I have frail-looking arms and legs and carry most of my weight in my trunk. With waist cinchers and girdles, I managed to compress and rearrange my fat well enough to get into clothes that otherwise might have been far too small. I was lucky that Europeans like voluptuous women—because in New York it's a completely different story. A model has to be sleek as a cat. After a few tough weeks of pounding the pavements, I realized that if I sought to be successful in the Big Apple, I had to lose weight and lose it fast. That's how I developed my Hummingbird Diet.

When someone asks me what I recommend for my models and friends who wish to reduce sensibly, I give her my own personal diet scheme and tell her how to follow it.

To stay on a diet takes tremendous willpower, and I have enough for three people, but I don't have too much time. The Hummingbird Diet grew out of my need to get thin without giving weight loss too much attention or forethought. A quarter of an hour a day was about all I could squeeze into my busy model's existence. I've got that down to thirteen minutes now, and that's all the time you need for planning and maintaining my delicious, nutritious Hummingbird Diet.

Good nutrition is the best basic "makeup" a model can use. Real beauty starts with her muscle, bone, hair and skin cells. There's no such thing as a gaunt, run-down, undernourished glamour girl. People may lose weight on crash programs, and there isn't a dieter in the world who doesn't have a pet torture: three bananas and a glass of skim milk three times a day; the rice diet; eight glasses of water and an exclusive intake of low-carbohydrate foods. They all work for short bursts of time, but for permanent weight loss, not on your life. And did you ever ask your doctor or a nutritionist what he thinks of such one-shot weight reducers? I myself have crash-dieted in an emergency before an important photo assignment; but for keeping myself in perfect trim on a timesaving day-by-day basis, nothing has ever made as much sense as my thirteen-minute-a-day Hummingbird routine.

Where did the name come from? From those oft-uttered words "I eat like a bird, but I still gain weight." We all say it. It's an automatic reflex for the overweight, and the truth is, most people *do* eat like humming-birds: those charming little creatures never stop eating. So while you're examining yourself, your self-image, accepting the physical type you are instead of trying to pattern yourself after the physical types you are not and never can be, remember that my gorgeous models also fight the battle of the bulge. Their problem is compounded by crazy working hours that lead to even crazier eating patterns.

You'll note that these hours are not too different from those of busy nonmodels like yourself.

If you're a homemaker, you're up at the crack of dawn getting breakfast for a departing spouse and a couple of schoolchildren who have to be put together with box lunches and sporting equipment. Beds have to be made, floors vacuumed; the larder has to be kept in good order. There are the car pool, PTA, League of Women Voters; early-morning phone calls; a coffee break at nine-thirty and an endless round of chores until nighttime comes and the last dinner dish is washed and stacked in the cupboard.

If you're a career woman, you put in a day of equally tension-filled tasks that lead to compensatory grabbing of quick meals. There is the same early rising, limited time for dressing and makeup, a quick cup of something hot, the race for the train or bus, early meetings, office work, a fast sandwich at the desk—or what is often more tiring, a lunch hour jammed with errands followed by a very rich business lunch that leaves you groggy and wanting to dash to the nearest easy chair for a catnap. There is the usual mountain of phone calls, and round about four in the afternoon that insatiable desire to absolutely have something to eat to break the dizzy pace—something that usually is no good for the waistline. At the end of the day, too tired to eat a full meal, you may still have to prepare food for a few friends you've invited in for dinner.

And so the skirmish goes on. No matter what our life-style. We are members of a vast legion of potential "fatties." We're all in it together—homemakers, career women and models. So my advice to every hopeful beauty is, try my Hummingbird Diet. The challenge is to count calories, keep track of them and burn up the excess fat reserve without depriving your brain, skin, eyes, hair, teeth and the rest of you of the nutrients they need for perfect health and glowing good looks.

SEVEN BASIC FOODS

My Hummingbird Diet is built on low-calorie arrangements of the seven basic foods that should be in every daily diet. It provides all the essentials for beauty and includes milk; eggs; butter; whole-grain and enriched bread and cereal foods; meat, fish or poultry; fruits and vegetables. To guarantee that you're eating at least the minimum requirement, you should be sure to have the following foods every single day, without fail: one pint of milk; one egg; one tablespoon of butter; three slices of bread; one serving of meat, fish or poultry; one citrus fruit or tomato and one serving of a green leafy or yellow vegetable. When you are on the Hummingbird Diet you should be able to adhere to this minimum without difficulty. For example: one pint of milk (skim or buttermilk) has 174 calories; a pat of butter, 100 calories; an egg, boiled or poached, has

77 calories; three slices of whole-wheat bread have 165 calories. That adds up to 516 calories. If you're on a 1200-calorie-per-day diet, you would still have 684 calories to budget on your fruit; vegetables; meat, fish or poultry; dessert and beverage.

This seven-basics low-calorie approach to Hummingbird eating makes good sense for everyone. It's a filling diet that leaves room for interesting variety and plenty of beauty nutrients.

Here's where these nutrients are found.

PROTEIN

It's about as impossible to have a beautiful body without protein as it is to make a soufflé without eggs. Proteins are what our muscle, bone, organ, skin, hair and nail cells are made of. Without protein, muscles lose their tone, organs become sluggish because of poor internal muscle tone, skin looks coarse and saggy and hair grows dull and scraggly. That's why models count on protein as the mainstay of their diet. It means eating lots of whole-protein foods like eggs, cheese, milk, poultry, meat and fish. To determine how much protein you need to keep your cells in tip-top condition, divide the number of pounds in your *desired* body weight (see the chart on page 36) in half: that's the number of grams of protein from whole-protein foods you'll need. Though some cereals and vegetables contain incomplete protein grams, they don't enter into this count because they need other proteins before they can be fully utilized.

CARBOHYDRATES

These include starches and sugars like bread, pasta, potatoes, sweets and soft drinks. Carbohydrates are necessary for energy. In a reducing diet carbohydrates are almost completely eliminated because energy can be drawn from abundant accumulated fat cells. Generally models eat a minimum of carbohydrates whether they are fighting off pounds or not—because most foods, even high-protein foods, have some carbohydrate value. Beware! If you have no accumulated fat to draw upon, energy will be stolen from protein needed for cell repair, and that can be dangerous.

FATS

Models can't afford to be fat, but that doesn't mean they don't consume fats. They just keep their intake to a minimum and generally stick to unsaturated fats (those which are liquid at room temperature) because they aren't as likely to cause the skin problems solid fats like butter, meat fat and chocolate often do. Some fat is essential for quick energy, the body's chemical balance, healthy skin and the thin protective cushion under the skin.

VITAMINS

These are found in small quantities in all foods—proteins, carbohydrates and fats. They're necessary for overall health and beauty. Though a well-balanced diet usually contains sufficient amounts of all vitamins, a shortage can occur because vitamins can be lost through the processes of freezing and defrosting, peeling fruits and vegetables, letting them wilt, cooking in too much water or overcooking. One way to guard against a vitamin shortage is to use the cooking water in soups or a cocktail. Be sure you're eating enough of particular foods to get the vitamins your own body specially requires.

Vitamin A

This is a skin and eye vitamin. A deficiency could cause eye problems or make your skin look dry, tired and bumpy. It may even cause dandruff. To guard against this deficiency, eat plenty of green leafy vegetables, yellow vegetables, fruits, egg yolk, cheese, butter and whole milk.

Vitamin B_1 (thiamin)

This vitamin keeps both your nervous and your digestive systems in top shape, helps your body utilize carbohydrates for energy and helps prevent fatigue and irritability. It's found in organ meats, eggs, green leafy vegetables, pork and whole cereals.

Vitamin B_2 (riboflavin) and B_6

These are two skin vitamins. A vitamin B_2 shortage makes lips dry and causes greasy, crusty blotches of skin at the sides of the nose. It's found in milk, meat, eggs, green leafy vegetables, whole-grain and enriched bread and cereals, cheese and yogurt. Vitamin B_6 is essential for clear, healthy skin too. That's why liver, meat, green vegetables, eggs and milk are skin beauty foods.

Vitamin B_{12}

This is an antianemia vitamin and essential for rich, healthy blood. It's found in milk, organ meats, fish and yogurt.

Vitamin C

To build strong blood vessels and healthy gums, vitamin C is essential. It also helps the body resist infections and maintain teeth and bones and helps wounds heal quickly. Since it can't be stored, citrus fruits, tomatoes and/or green leafy vegetables should be in the daily diet.

Vitamin D

This is the tooth and bone vitamin, since it helps the body to use calcium and phosphorous, two strengthening minerals. It's found in eggs, fish, liver oils and fortified milk.

MINERALS

Besides calcium and phosphorous, there are two more beauty minerals: iron and iodine. Iron gives you blushed cheeks and lips and energy to live like a beauty. It's found in meat, green leafy vegetables, egg yolks, whole-grain bread and cereals and oysters. Iodine increases alertness and efficiency and promotes good circulation, which is vital to healthy skin and hair. It's found in seafood, salt-water fish and iodized salt.

These are the vitamins and minerals that go into the Hummingbird Diet. These, plus eight full glasses of water per day, can just about guarantee maximum health and beauty.

THE HUMMINGBIRD PRINCIPLE

Like the perpetual-motion hummingbird in search of the nectar that is the source of her boundless energy, a busy woman needs proper nutrition; but she needn't stick to the old-fashioned, time-consuming restriction of three square meals per day taken at three specific times of day. Not at all. It makes no difference if she eats like a hummingbird, flitting from food to food, many times per day, as long as she doesn't exceed the maximum number of calories to which she's made a commitment. Most of us can lose 1 to 2 pounds per week on a 1200-calorie-per-day limit without developing a sagging chin or a flabby abdomen. Try it yourself to prove the point. The Hummingbird Diet is the slow-but-sure way to keep pounds off. It takes patience and that willpower I spoke of, but it's worth both if you want to lose weight once and for all. The success of the Hummingbird Diet lies in the fact that it does more than just reduce you: it introduces your body to new eating habits based upon the scientific principles of good nutrition. It gives your body time to stabilize and balance itself chemically during your weight loss. And it's not so arduous a task when you consider that it keeps you from bouncing right back to the weight that disturbed you and brought you to the Hummingbird Diet in the first place.

So here's what you do.

See the Calorie Intake Calculator on page 114. Find your present weight in column one. Column two has the number of calories you have probably been eating each day to maintain your present weight. If you want to lose 1 pound a week, just cut 600 calories from that number (column three calculates that for you); if you wish to lose 2 pounds a week, cut 1200 calories (calculated for you in column four).

It really works. One of our young models who came from the Midwest was just about ready to pack up and go home. No agency would take her on because, though she was beautiful, she was 10 pounds too heavy. She had tried all sorts of diets but couldn't stick to them for more than a few pounds. As a final resort, she went to her doctor, who set up this diet for her. Since she weighed in at 135 pounds, she must have been eating 2025 calories a day. To lose 2 pounds a week at her weight, she'd have to cut down to 825 calories a day, and she knew from past experience that that would be too restricting for her—she'd probably start feeling deprived, then give up the whole thing before she reached her goal. So she decided on the 1-pound-a-week-off version. She ate 1425 calories per day and concentrated on eating a good portion of those calories in protein. It was practically painless. The first few weeks she lost even more weight than she had expected. After the first few pounds, she stopped losing for a week—that was when her body was adjusting chemically to its new weight. But because she had enough variety in her diet and understood the reason for the momentary standstill, she didn't become discouraged and give up as she had done before. Within two months she had lost all her extra pounds, and today, as a result of modifying her behavior, she is as slim as she needs to be to pursue her modeling career with great success.

You can get the same good results by following her example, adding one more very important element to the process. You budget your calories by writing them down after each meal or snack. That way you are in complete control of your own intake at all times. For example: By checking the Calorie Chart that begins on page 148, you see that you've

CALORIE INTAKE CALCULATOR

Present weight	Present daily intake* (total number of calories it takes to maintain present body weight)	Daily calories to lose 1 pound a week (600 calories a day less than present daily intake)	Daily calories to lose 2 pounds a week (1200 calories a day less than present daily intake)
250	3750	3150	2550
245	3675	3075	2475
240	3600	3000	2400
235	3525	2925	2325
230	3450	2850	2250
225	3375	2775	2175
220	3300	2700	2100
215	3225	2625	2025
210	3150	2550	1950
205	3075	2475	1875
200	3000	2400	1800
195	2925	2325	1725
190	2850	2250	1650
185	2775	2175	1575
180	2700	2100	1500
175	2625	2025	1425
170	2550	1950	1350
165	2475	1875	1275
160	2400	1800	1200
155	2325	1725	1125
150	2250	1650	1050
145	2175	1575	975
140	2100	1500	900
135	2025	1425	825
130	1950	1350	750
125	1875	1275	675
120	1800	1200	——
115	1725	1125	——
110	1650	1050	——
105	1575	975	——
100	1500	900	——

*Your weight $\times$ 15 = the number of calories that will maintain your present weight.

eaten 750 of your 1200-calorie allotment at breakfast and lunch. A glance at your notations will show you you have only 450 calories left for supper and a late-night refreshment. You can eat plenty of vegetables, an egg or some cheese or meat, a slice of whole-wheat bread, a portion of ice cream or ice milk and a cup of a beverage without going overboard.

So treat yourself to the Hummingbird habit.

Take ten minutes in the morning to look over the seven sample calorie-counted daily menus you'll find on pages 109–112. Choose an outline that suits your particular taste for the day, and stick to it. If you'd rather eat only your favorite foods, you can choose among the seven calorie-counted main dishes for which I've provided recipes as the focal point for your own low-calorie-menu composition. All boring no-nos have been eliminated; your menu includes a dessert! I've even suggested twenty-one additional delicious slim-maintenance desserts. No ridiculous time-wasting thumbing through diet books by the hour. You'll need only one more minute at the end of each meal to tally up the number of calories you've consumed. With common sense and only thirteen precious minutes per day you can safely lose 5 to 8 pounds in the first month. You can take off those pounds and keep them off on the Hummingbird Diet.

A FEW SIMPLE SUGGESTIONS TO FOLLOW

1. Plan meals that are nutritionally balanced and sound, using the information I've supplied on pages 109–112.

2. Eat whenever you're hungry, just as the Hummingbird does.

3. Keep a record of the calorie count each time you eat. Use a little pad or seven index cards fastened with a paper clip; either system works well if you want to repeat your own week's menus.

4. *Do not exceed the calorie limit you've set for yourself.* If you go overboard because you've been to a party, cut down for a couple of days until your average is reestablished—but don't quit.

5. Easy does it. Don't expect to be superhuman. You're the only one in the race, and guilt won't help. If you give up for a day or so, you won't lose too much ground. Just step right back to the starting gate and take off for the finish line you've put down for yourself.

The Hummingbird Diet becomes so natural after a week or two that you won't even have to think about it. Here are a few tricks that my models use to stay on the routines they've set up. You might like to try them.

MODELS' DIET TRICKS

Just as great cooks have their culinary secrets, successful models have a list of confidential methods covering all sorts of dieting situations. The same tricks don't work for everyone. Experiment to find your own special combinations. These "secrets" are just plain common sense, but they're all worth trying until you find the ones that really work for you. One of the most difficult mechanisms, but one of the most useful, is convincing yourself you don't want—even that you don't like—weight-producing goodies. When your extra pounds are gone, you may find that your capacity for these rich things has diminished. You may even invent a few tricks of your own and write them down next to any of the following suggestions that make sense to your own way of thinking. After all, your own personal methods will serve you best.

SLIM SHOPPING

1. Never go shopping for groceries when you're hungry—it is preferable to go just after you've eaten a meal.

2. Make a list of essentials (again, when you're not hungry) and promise yourself not to buy one thing that's not on the list. Stick to your promise. That way you won't be likely to pick up a package of cookies or a candy bar on impulse.

3. Avoid buying anything labeled "dietetic" unless you check its calorie content first and compare it with the nondietetic food. It may not be lower in calories—it may be labeled dietetic because it's designed for persons on special diets for reasons of health.

4. Buy water-packed rather than oil-packed fish, water-packed rather than syrup-packed fruits.

5. Stock up on seasonal fresh vegetables and experiment with them in unusual recipes (without lots of butter or cream sauces, though). Cooking and eating should be a new nonfattening adventure.

6. Buy seasonal fruits as treats instead of rich desserts.

7. Once you've procured everything on your list, leave the market quickly. Don't stick around to tempt yourself.

SLIM AROUND THE HOUSE

If you're at home all day and/or all night with a full refrigerator at your disposal, you really have to use all your willpower. Here are a few suggestions that will help you to strengthen your determination.

1. If you're a "secret food snitcher," try not to eat alone. This isn't practical if you live by yourself, but if you have someone else around, it really works.

2. Resolve to eat only when you are sitting down. No more head-in-the-refrigerator snacking.

3. Learn to smell the right seasoning balance rather than tasting for it—this is the way really good chefs do it anyway.

4. No more bowl licking or cleaning the last spoonful off the baby's plate. Adding 33 calories per meal each day can amount to 10 pounds in one year.

5. Prepare a supply of raw vegetables—carrots, celery, radishes and so on—and keep them in your refrigerator at all times for quick pickups. (But remember to sit down when eating them.)

6. If fear motivates you best, paste a picture of a very fat person inside your refrigerator door and cabinets; if vanity motivates you, paste a picture of a beautiful slim model in the same places. Or try contrasting pictures: dieting requires a sense of humor.

7. Keep busy around the house—read, sew, start a decorating project. Do anything to keep your mind out of the kitchen.

SLIM PARTYING

1. If you've lost weight, take in your party dresses—you'll look better and you won't be as likely to fill them out again.

2. Stand clear of snacking areas. It's all too easy to reach automatically into the bowl of peanuts or popcorn at your elbow. Just one move and you're hooked.

3. Avoid partaking of the hors d'oeuvre if possible. Once you start, it's hard to stop.

4. If you must munch, allow yourself only rabbit-patch foods like carrots, celery and the like—or high-protein things like shrimp, cheese and so on. Dips, crackers, bread, chips, pretzels or nuts—not allowed.

5. Try not to use up your dinner calories early in the evening. Save most of them for dinner and leave a few for later on, if you get hungry.

6. Learn to get mileage from one drink. Keep adding ice, soda or water to your glass. Alcohol is nutritionally empty but relatively high in calories. If you keep your hands busy with one watered-down drink, you won't feel deprived.

7. *Never* talk about diet—it's boring to you and everyone else. Besides, if you don't mention the word, people aren't as likely to notice you need one.

SLIM EATING OUT

1. It is unwise to go out to dine with the idea of giving up your diet. If you approach your evening that way, you'll probably end up doing just that.

2. If you have a choice of menu, stick to chicken or fish dishes prepared without rich sauces.

3. Avoid bread, potatoes and rich desserts. Fill up with vegetables and finish off your meal with a succulent fresh fruit.

4. It's a good idea to eat your salad *before* the main course. Lemon juice or vinegar, salt and pepper are all you need to spark up a salad. Avoid rich dressings.

5. If you're someplace where you don't have a choice and fattening foods are served, eat only *half* of the portion. No one will consider you impolite, if you're consistent throughout the meal.

6. Pass up seconds—eat slowly and you won't have to explain why.

PLATEAU TRICKS

The hardest moment in the life of a dieter is that moment when the scale doesn't seem to budge even though she's followed her diet down to the last calorie. It happens to just about anybody in just about any diet, but it's only temporary. Resolve to stay with it. With a few boosts for the morale you can get through it without giving up.

1. Buy a dress in the size you *want* to be.

2. Alter all the clothes in your closet—you'll feel good about your progress up to that point, and you won't want to let the garments out again.

3. Pamper yourself a little—try a new haircut; get a trim or a restyling.

4. Experiment with new makeup. Play up your newly exposed bone structure with shadow and color.

5. Promise yourself some sort of treat—a reward—when you lose the next pound. Set a new goal. One pound at a time won't seem impossible. Once you lose that 1 more pound, you're on your way back to losing again. The obstacle of the diet plateau will have been surmounted.

You will find the next several pages most helpful. They list Hummingbird diets for a full week, offer specific recipes for special slimming dishes, and, finally, provide an extensive calorie and gram chart.

HUMMINGBIRD DIET

Day #1

7:30 A.M.   I orange
1/4 cup cottage cheese
coffee or tea

11:00 A.M.   I slice toast
I tablespoon jam
coffee or tea

12:30 P.M.   1/2 cup cream of asparagus soup
I pear
coffee or tea

2:30 P.M.   31/2 ounces water-packed tuna
I tablespoon diet mayonnaise
I slice toast
coffee or tea

4:30 P.M.   1/2 cup ice milk

6:00 P.M.   **DIVINE CHICKEN***
I cup spinach
1/2 teaspoon diet margarine
6 whole asparagus spears
coffee or tea

8:00 P.M.   **GRENADA CHEESECAKE***
coffee or tea

10:00 P.M.   1/2 cup ice milk

*Recipes on pages 127–128.

The Hummingbird Diet: Eating for Beauty

Day #2

7:30 A.M.	1/2 cup orange juice
	1 slice pumpernickel toast
	1 teaspoon diet margarine
	coffee or tea

9:00 A.M.	1 poached egg
	1/2 water bagel
	1 teaspoon diet margarine
	coffee or tea

11:00 A.M.	1/2 water bagel
	1 teaspoon diet margarine
	coffee or tea

12:30 P.M.	2 ounces chopped chicken liver
	1 slice rye toast
	lettuce and onion salad
	lemon juice for salad dressing
	coffee or tea

| 3:00 P.M. | cup of strawberries |

6:00 P.M.	SHASHLIK*
	1 cup carrots
	1 teaspoon diet margarine
	coffee or tea

| 8:00 P.M. | PECAN BROWNIE* |
| | coffee or tea |

| 10:00 P.M. | 1/4 cup ice milk |
| | 1/2 cantaloupe |

*Recipes on pages 128–129.

Day #3

7:00 A.M.	1 slice Italian bread 1 teaspoon diet margarine coffee or tea
8:00 A.M.	1 fried egg 1 teaspoon diet margarine 1 slice diet whole-wheat bread coffee or tea
11:00 A.M.	1 cup minestrone soup
12:30 P.M.	1 slice Italian bread lettuce, onion and green pepper salad lemon juice for salad dressing coffee or tea
3:00 P.M.	1 tortoni
6:00 P.M.	ROSEMARY CHICKEN* ½ cup spaghetti with tomato sauce 1 cup kale
8:00 P.M.	MOCHA PUDDING PIE* coffee or tea
10:00 P.M.	1 slice Italian bread 1 ounce sliced Provolone coffee or tea

*Recipes on pages 129–130.

Day #4

8:00 A.M. I orange
           coffee or tea

9:30 A.M. I slice wheat-soya bread
           I tablespoon honey
           coffee or tea

12:00 NOON I cup split-pea soup
           I pear
           coffee or tea

3:00 P.M. I slice whole-wheat bread
           I tablespoon peanut butter
           coffee or tea

6:00 P.M. ORIENTAL BEEF AND BEANS*
           I salad (½ apple, ½ banana, I ounce sunflower seeds)
           lemon juice for salad dressing
           coffee or tea

9:00 P.M. HARD LABOR LIME PIE*
           coffee or tea

10:00 P.M. ¼ cup raisins

*Recipes on pages 130–131.

Day #5

8:00 A.M. ½ apple
2 tablespoons cottage cheese
coffee or tea

10:00 A.M. I hard-boiled egg
I slice whole-wheat diet bread
I teaspoon jam
coffee or tea

12:00 NOON 2 slices bacon, well drained
I slice diet-bread toast
I sliced tomato
I tablespoon diet mayonnaise
coffee or tea

3:00 P.M. I tangerine

6:00 P.M. ROAST DUCK*
½ baked acorn squash
¼ head of lettuce
lemon juice for salad dressing
coffee or tea

8:00 P.M. COFFEE SOUFFLE*
coffee or tea

10:00 P.M. I cup fresh strawberries
½ cup skim milk

*Recipes on pages 131–132.

Day #6

8:00 A.M.   1 orange
1 poached egg
1 slice diet-bread toast
1/2 teaspoon diet margarine
   coffee or tea

10:00 A.M.   1 slice diet-bread toast
1 teaspoon jam
   coffee or tea

12:20 P.M.   1 slice diet-bread toast
1 slice Swiss cheese
   lettuce leaves
1 teaspoon diet mayonnaise
1/4 cup coleslaw
   coffee or tea

3:00 P.M.   1/2 cup ice milk

6:30 P.M.   MUSTARD SAUCE CHICKEN*
3/4 cup fresh green beans
1/2 head lettuce
   lemon juice for salad dressing
   coffee or tea

8:00 P.M.   MISS LUCY'S BANANA TREAT*
   coffee or tea

10:00 P.M.   1/4 cup ice milk
1 plain sugar cookie
   tea

*Recipes on page 133.

Day #7

8:00 A.M.   ½ grapefruit
             I slice diet-bread toast
             I teaspoon diet margarine
             coffee or tea

10:00 A.M.   I cup skim milk
             I slice diet-bread toast
             ½ teaspoon butter
             I teaspoon jam

12:30 P.M.   Open-faced liverwurst sandwich (2 ounces liverwurst,
             I slice rye bread, mustard)
             I apple
             coffee or tea

3:00 P.M.   I sliced peach
             I cup yogurt

6:00 P.M.   VEAL SCALOPPINE au MARSALA*
             10 asparagus spears
             I teaspoon diet margarine
             coffee or tea

8:00 P.M.   SPONGE CAKE WITH BLUEBERRIES*
             coffee or tea

10:00 P.M.   ¼ cup ice milk

*Recipes on page 134.

RECIPES FOR THE HUMMINGBIRD DIET

Divine Chicken

4 tablespoons flour, divided
½ teaspoon salt
¼ teaspoon ground pepper
2 tablespoons vegetable oil
4 chicken-breast halves

1 package (10 oz.) frozen broccoli
½ cup chicken consommé
½ cup milk
½ teaspoon crumbled tarragon
2 tablespoons bread crumbs

Combine 2 tablespoons flour, salt and pepper. Heat oil in Dutch oven. Coat chicken with seasoned flour. Brown chicken in hot oil. Reduce heat, cover and cook 30 minutes. Add broccoli last 15 minutes of cooking time. Remove chicken and broccoli to heatproof platter and keep warm.

Stir 2 tablespoons of flour into sauce. Add consommé, milk and tarragon. Cook and stir sauce until thickened. Pour sauce over chicken and broccoli. Sprinkle with bread crumbs, then brown under broiler.

Yield: 4 servings
250 calories per serving

Grenada Cheese Cake

2 envelopes unflavored gelatin
1 cup reliquefied nonfat
  dry milk
4 eggs, separated
  nonnutritive sweetener
  equivalent to 1¼ cups sugar
¼ teaspoon salt
1 teaspoon grated orange rind
1 teaspoon grated lime rind

1 tablespoon lime juice
1½ teaspoons vanilla
½ teaspoon almond extract
3 cups creamed cottage cheese
½ teaspoon cream of tartar
⅓ cup graham-cracker crumbs
⅛ teaspoon each cinnamon
  and nutmeg

Sprinkle gelatin over milk in top of double boiler. Add egg yolks. Stir until completely blended. Place over hot water. Stir constantly until gelatin dissolves and mixture thickens slightly—about 5 minutes. Remove from heat. Stir in artificial sweetener, salt, grated orange and lime rinds, lime juice, vanilla and almond extract.

Place cottage cheese in electric blender and turn to high speed, blending until cottage cheese is smooth—3 or 4 minutes. Stir cottage cheese into gelatin mixture. Chill, stirring occasionally, until mixture mounds slightly when dropped from a spoon.

Beat egg whites and cream of tartar until very stiff. Fold into gelatin mixture.

Combine graham-cracker crumbs, cinnamon and nutmeg. Sprinkle half of crumbs over bottom of 8- or 9-inch springform pan. Turn gelatin mixture into pan and cover with remaining crumbs. Chill until firm.

Yield: 12 servings
96 calories per serving

Shashlik

1 pound boneless leg of lamb, cut into 1-inch cubes	2 green peppers, cut into 12 squares
1 cup low-calorie Italian salad dressing	1/2 cup ketchup
2 bay leaves	1 teaspoon Worcestershire
12 mushroom caps	1/4 teaspoon Tabasco
	2 tomatoes, cut into quarters

Place meat in large bowl. Combine low-calorie dressing and bay leaves. Pour over lamb. Place lamb in refrigerator; chill overnight, turning occasionally. Drain lamb and reserve marinade.

Divide lamb into four portions. Place lamb on skewers, alternating lamb with mushroom caps and pepper squares. Brush lamb and vegetables with marinade. Broil shashlik 15 minutes, basting with marinade.

Combine ketchup, Worcestershire and Tabasco. Remove shashlik from broiler. Place tomato quarters on ends of skewers. Brush shashlik with ketchup sauce. Broil shashlik 5 to 10 minutes or until tender.

Yield: 4 servings
166 calories per serving

Pecan Brownies

⅔ cup sifted cake flour	I cup brown sugar
I teaspoon baking powder	I egg
½ teaspoon salt	½ cup chopped pecans
¼ cup butter	I teaspoon vanilla

Sift together flour, baking powder and salt. Combine butter and sugar. Add egg and beat well. Stir in pecans and vanilla. Mix in dry ingredients. Turn into greased 8-inch-square baking pan. Bake in 350°F. oven for 25 to 30 minutes. Cut into 2-inch squares while warm.

Yield: 16 squares
125 calories per square

Rosemary Chicken

¼ cup vegetable oil	½ cup chopped onion
I broiler/fryer (2½ to	I cup chopped celery
3 pounds), cut into quarters	¼ cup dry sherry
I teaspoon salt	1½ teaspoons rosemary
¼ teaspoon ground pepper	

Heat oil in Dutch oven. Brown chicken. Drain off oil except for 2 table-spoons. Sprinkle chicken with salt and pepper. Add remaining ingredients. Cover and simmer 30 minutes, basting occasionally.

Yield: 4 servings
280 calories per serving

Mocha Pudding Pie

3 cups breakfast wheat flakes
1 tablespoon butter
2 tablespoons brown sugar

2 envelopes low-calorie chocolate
  pudding mix
2 cups skim milk
2 tablespoons instant coffee

Crush wheat flakes into crumbs. Combine wheat-flake crumbs, butter and brown sugar. Press crumb mixture onto bottom and sides of 8-inch pie pan. Bake in 375°F. oven for 8 minutes. Cool pie shell while making filling.

Combine pudding mix, skim milk and instant coffee in a 2-quart saucepan. Heat and stir until mixture boils. Cool mixture and allow to thicken. Pour mixture into piecrust. Chill until firm.

Yield: 8 servings
90 calories per serving

Oriental Beef and Beans

2 tablespoons peanut oil
1/2 pound beef, cut into strips
1/2 cup chopped onion
1 cup cut green beans
1 green pepper, sliced
1 cup sliced celery

4 teaspoons cornstarch
1 tablespoon soy sauce
3/4 cup water
1/2 teaspoon salt
1/4 teaspoon ground pepper
1/2 pound mushrooms, sliced

Heat oil in heavy skillet. Brown meat in oil, stirring occasionally. Add onions, beans, green pepper and celery. Cook 4 to 5 minutes.

Combine cornstarch, soy sauce, water, salt and ground pepper. Add to skillet and mix thoroughly. Add mushrooms, stirring constantly. Cook and stir until sauce is clear.

Yield: 4 servings
230 calories per serving

Hard Labor Lime Pie

Crust:
  1 cup dry rye-bread crumbs
  2 tablespoons brown sugar
  1/4 teaspoon salt
  1/8 teaspoon ground nutmeg
  1 tablespoon butter
Filling:
  1 envelope unflavored gelatin
  1/4 cup sugar
  1/8 teaspoon salt
  1/2 cup buttermilk
  1 teaspoon finely grated
    lime rind
  3 tablespoons lime juice
  1 1/2 cups sieved uncreamed
    cottage cheese
  1 egg white, beaten stiff

Combine bread crumbs, sugar, salt, nutmeg and butter. Stir to blend well. Press crumb mixture onto bottom and sides of 8-inch pie pan. Bake in 375°F. oven for 8 minutes. Cool before filling.

Mix gelatin, sugar and salt in top of double boiler. Add buttermilk and cook over boiling water for about 8 minutes, stirring constantly. Cool. Stir in lime rind, lime juice and cottage cheese. Place mixture in blender and blend for a minute to achieve smoothness of texture. Chill.

Fold in egg white when mixture begins to thicken. Pour into crust. Chill several hours before serving.

Yield: 8 servings
125 calories per serving

Roast Duck

  1 duck, 4 to 5 pounds
  1 teaspoon garlic salt
  4 oranges, cut into quarters
  1/4 cup dry sherry
  1 teaspoon soy sauce
  1/4 teaspoon chopped ginger

Preheat oven to 325°F. Sprinkle duck with garlic salt. Fill cavity with orange quarters. Place duck breast side up on a high rack in roasting pan. Roast uncovered 2½ to 3 hours.

Combine sherry, soy sauce and ginger in saucepan. Bring to a boil, then remove from heat. Brush duck with sauce the last ½ hour of roasting. Remove duck from oven. Remove orange quarters and discard. Serve cut in quarters.

Yield: 4 servings
352 calories per serving

Coffee Soufflé

sugar	¾ cup skim milk
4 egg yolks	2 teaspoons cornstarch
2 tablespoons instant coffee	I tablespoon water
2 teaspoons vanilla extract	5 egg whites
butter	⅓ cup heavy cream, whipped
3 tablespoons flour	

Preheat oven to 350°F. Butter the bottom and sides of 2-quart casserole or soufflé dish. Sprinkle inside with sugar and then shake out excess.

Place egg yolks, ⅓ cup sugar, instant coffee and vanilla in mixing bowl. Beat until light and fluffy.

Melt 2 tablespoons butter in saucepan. Add flour and mix until smooth, stirring constantly. Add milk while continuing to stir. Cook until mixture thickens.

Mix cornstarch with water to make a smooth paste. Add to flour mixture, stirring constantly. Heat to a boil. Remove from heat.

Stir the egg-yolk mixture into saucepan until smooth.

Beat egg whites until stiff but not dry. Add about half of egg whites to sauce. Stir until smooth. Fold combined sauce into remaining half of egg whites.

Turn into buttered casserole or soufflé dish. Bake 45 to 50 minutes or until top is brown and soufflé is firm. Serve topped with whipped cream.

Yield: 6 servings
200 calories per serving

Mustard Sauce Chicken

1/4 cup flour
1/2 teaspoon salt
1/4 teaspoon garlic salt
1/4 teaspoon onion salt
4 chicken-breast halves
2 tablespoons vegetable oil

1 cup chicken consommé
1/2 tablespoon lemon juice
3/4 teaspoon dry mustard
1 tablespoon brown sugar
1/2 tablespoon cornstarch

Combine flour and salts. Sprinkle chicken with flour-and-salt mixture. Pour oil into Dutch oven and heat. Sauté chicken for about 5 minutes on each side. Add consommé and simmer 20 minutes.

Combine lemon juice, mustard, sugar and cornstarch to make a smooth paste. Remove chicken to hot serving platter when done. Add lemon-and-mustard paste to chicken sauce in Dutch oven. Stir sauce and cook until thickened. Pour sauce over chicken on platter.

Yield: 4 servings
260 calories per serving

Miss Lucy's Banana Treat

1 1/2 tablespoons butter
3 bananas, sliced lengthwise

1 1/2 tablespoons brown sugar
1 teaspoon lime juice

Heat butter in skillet. Brown bananas in butter. Turn bananas. Sprinkle with brown sugar and lime juice.

Yield: 6 servings
85 calories per serving

Veal Scaloppine au Marsala

1/2 teaspoon salt	I pound veal round,
1/4 teaspoon fresh ground pepper	cut in 1/4-inch-thick slices
I tablespoon flour	1/4 cup vegetable oil
	1/2 cup Marsala wine

Combine salt, pepper and flour. Sprinkle meat with flour mixture on both sides. Pound meat with mallet or flat of cleaver until meat is thin. Heat oil in skillet. Sauté veal over medium heat for 3 to 4 minutes on each side. Add wine. Simmer uncovered 10 minutes or until tender.

Yield: 4 servings
225 calories per serving

Sponge Cake with Blueberries

6 eggs	I cup sifted cake flour
I cup sugar	I 10-ounce package frozen
1/2 cup nonfat dry milk powder	blueberries, thawed
1/2 teaspoon salt	1/2 cup grape juice
I tablespoon lime juice	confectioner's sugar

Preheat oven to 350°F.

Place eggs, sugar, milk powder, salt and lime juice in large mixing bowl. Beat mixture at high speed until soft peaks form—about 15 to 20 minutes. Change mixer to low speed. Beat flour 1 tablespoon at a time into egg mixture. Pour batter into prepared 10-inch tube pan. Place pan in oven and bake for 45 minutes or until surface of cake is springy.

Remove cake from oven and place pan upside down on neck of a bottle to cool. Transfer cake to cake dish when cool. Combine blueberries and grape juice. Spoon blueberries in juice over top of cake. Sprinkle cake with confectioner's sugar.

Yield: 16 servings
145 calories per serving

21 MORE FAVORITE LOW-CALORIE DESSERTS

Fashion Show

1 cup low-fat cottage cheese	1/2 teaspoon grated orange rind
2 teaspoons chopped	2 bananas
candied ginger	1 cup strawberries, orange
2 teaspoons brown sugar	sections or pineapple cubes

Place cottage cheese in blender container, cover and process until smooth. If the cottage cheese is so dry that it will not puree in the blender, add 1 or 2 tablespoons of milk. Turn into medium bowl. Add ginger, brown sugar and orange rind. Cover and chill.

Peel and slice bananas and combine with other fruit in bowl or dessert dishes when ready to serve. Top with sauce.

Yield: 4 servings
100 calories per serving

Chilled Apricot Mousse

2 envelopes unflavored gelatin	1 tablespoon imitation brandy
1/2 cup cold water	flavoring
3/4 cup boiling water	1 cup diced dietetic-packed
2/3 cup nonfat dry milk powder	apricots, drained
nonnutritive sweetener	6 ice cubes
equivalent to 1/2 cup sugar	

Sprinkle gelatin over cold water in a 5-cup blender container and allow to soften while assembling other ingredients. Pour boiling water into blender. Cover; process at low speed until gelatin is dissolved. If gelatin granules cling to container, use a rubber spatula to push them into mixture. Add nonfat dry milk, sweetener and brandy flavoring. Process at low speed until well blended. Add apricots. Process at low, then high speed until well blended. Add ice cubes, one at a time, and process at high speed until ice is melted. Pour into sherbet glasses or compote dishes and chill.

Yield: 5 servings
approximately 88 calories per serving

Bordeaux Mountain Dessert

2 envelopes unflavored gelatin
$\frac{1}{2}$ cup cold water
$\frac{1}{2}$ cup lemon juice
   nonnutritive sweetener
   equivalent to 1 cup sugar
2 cups noncaloric ginger ale,
   stirred vigorously until all
   carbonation disappears

$\frac{1}{2}$ medium cantaloupe, diced or
   cut into balls
1 wedge (2 inches) honeydew
   melon, diced or cut into balls

Sprinkle gelatin over cold water in saucepan. Place over low heat and stir until gelatin dissolves—about 3 minutes. Remove from heat and add lemon juice, nonnutritive sweetener and ginger ale. Chill until mixture is consistency of unbeaten egg white. Fold in melon balls. Turn into 4-cup mold. Chill until firm. Unmold to serve. Garnish with additional melon balls and fresh mint if desired.

Yield: 6 servings
30 calories per serving

Ms. Lemon Peach

2 envelopes unflavored gelatin
   nonnutritive sweetener
   equivalent to $\frac{2}{3}$ cup sugar
3 cups cold water, divided

$\frac{1}{4}$ teaspoon salt
$\frac{1}{2}$ cup lemon juice
4 large peaches, sliced
   mint leaves

Mix together unflavored gelatin and sweetener in saucepan. Stir in 1½ cups cold water. Place over low heat. Stir until gelatin dissolves. Remove from heat. Stir in salt and lemon juice. Add remaining 1½ cups water. Pour into 4-cup ring mold. Chill until firm. Unmold and fill center of mold with sliced peaches. Garnish with mint.

Yield: 8 servings
28 calories per serving

Sauterne Zabaglione

5 egg yolks	1 tablespoon fresh lime juice
1 whole egg	½ teaspoon ginger
¼ cup sugar	8 fresh nectarines, peeled
½ cup Sauterne	and sliced

Beat yolks and whole egg in large mixer bowl until thick. Beat in sugar gradually. Beat until mixture is light and tripled in bulk. Beat in Sauterne, lime juice and ginger slowly. Pour mixture into top of double boiler. Place over simmering water. Beat with rotary beater or electric mixer until light and frothy, the consistency of whipped cream—about 8 minutes. Pour over sliced nectarines in dessert dishes.

Yield: 8 servings
125 calories per serving

Molded Lime Chiffon Fruit

1 envelope unflavored gelatin	1¾ cups skim milk
2 tablespoons plus ¼ cup sugar, divided	2 teaspoons grated lime rind
⅛ teaspoon salt	2 tablespoons lime juice
2 eggs, separated	2 cans (8 ounces each) water-pack fruit cocktail, well drained

Mix gelatin, 2 tablespoons sugar and salt in saucepan. Beat together egg yolks and milk in bowl. Stir into gelatin mixture. Place over low heat.

Stir constantly until gelatin dissolves and mixture thickens slightly—about 5 minutes. Remove from heat. Stir in lime rind and lime juice. Chill, stirring occasionally, until mixture mounds slightly when dropped from a spoon.

Beat egg whites in small mixing bowl until soft peaks form; gradually beat in remaining ¼ cup sugar and beat until stiff but not dry. Fold egg whites and fruit cocktail into gelatin mixture. Turn into 6-cup mold. Chill until set. Unmold and garnish with additional fruit, if desired.

Yield: 8 servings
100 calories per serving

Willy's Lemon Mousse

2 envelopes unflavored gelatin	2 teaspoons grated lemon rind
2½ cups water, divided	½ cup nonfat dry milk powder
½ cup plus 1 tablespoon lemon juice, divided	½ cup ice water
nonnutritive sweetener equivalent to 1 cup sugar	fresh strawberries for garnish

Sprinkle gelatin over ½ cup water in saucepan to soften. Place over low heat and stir constantly until gelatin dissolves—about 2 to 3 minutes. Remove from heat. Stir in ½ cup lemon juice, remaining 2 cups water, nonnutritive sweetener and lemon rind. Chill until mixture is consistency of unbeaten egg white.

Beat nonfat dry milk with ice water and remaining 1 tablespoon lemon juice until soft peaks form. Beat in lemon mixture gradually until volume increases and mixture is light and fluffy. Turn into an 8-cup mold. Chill until firm. Unmold and garnish with strawberries.

Yield: 12 servings
18 calories per serving

Bruce's Lemon Chiffon Pie

1 envelope unflavored gelatin	1/8 teaspoon salt
1/2 cup lemon juice	4 eggs, separated
1/4 cup water	1 teaspoon grated lemon rind
nonnutritive sweetener	1/4 cup sugar
equivalent to 3/4 cup sugar	1 9-inch crumb crust*

Sprinkle gelatin on lemon juice in top of double boiler. Add water, sweetener and salt. Beat egg yolks; stir into mixture and blend well. Place over boiling water and cook, stirring constantly, until gelatin dissolves and mixture thickens slightly—3 or 4 minutes. Remove from heat; stir in lemon rind. Chill, stirring occasionally, until mixture mounds slightly when dropped from a spoon.

Beat egg whites until stiff, but not dry. Add sugar gradually and beat until very stiff. Fold in gelatin mixture. Turn into prepared piecrust; chill until firm.

Yield: 6 servings
169 calories per serving

*CRUMB CRUST

2 tablespoons melted butter	2/3 cup cornflake crumbs

Combine butter and cornflake crumbs. Press into bottom and sides of 9-inch pie plate.

Maui Torte

1 envelope unflavored gelatin
1/4 cup sugar
1/4 teaspoon salt
3 eggs, separated
1 1/4 cups canned crushed
   pineapple and syrup

1 tablespoon lemon juice
1/2 cup ice water
1/2 cup instant nonfat dry
   milk powder
4 chocolate cookie wafers

Mix together gelatin, sugar and salt in saucepan. Beat egg yolks slightly; stir in pineapple and syrup. Add to gelatin mixture and cook over low heat, stirring constantly, until gelatin dissolves and mixture thickens slightly—5 to 8 minutes. Remove from heat; stir in lemon juice. Chill until mixture is the consistency of unbeaten egg white.

Beat egg whites until stiff, but not dry; fold in gelatin mixture.

Beat ice water and instant nonfat dry milk powder with electric mixer or rotary beater until stiff. Fold into gelatin mixture.

Spoon 1/3 of the mixture into a 9×5×3-inch loaf pan; top with 2 large thin chocolate wafers, whole or in crumbs. Repeat, ending with gelatin mixture. Chill until firm. Unmold, and if desired, garnish with additional cookie crumbs or whipped-milk topping.

Yield: 10 servings
114 calories per serving

Peaches and Cheese Treat

1 envelope unflavored gelatin
1/2 cup sugar, divided
2 eggs, separated
3/4 cup skim milk
1/8 teaspoon salt

1/2 teaspoon grated lemon rind
1 1/2 teaspoons lemon juice
1/2 teaspoon vanilla
1 1/2 cups creamed cottage cheese
2 cups diced fresh peaches

Mix gelatin and 1/4 cup sugar in saucepan. Beat egg yolks with milk and stir into gelatin mixture. Place over low heat; stir constantly until gelatin dissolves and mixture thickens slightly—about 5 minutes. Remove from heat; add salt, lemon rind, lemon juice and vanilla.

Sieve cottage cheese or beat at high speed of electric mixer until smooth; stir into gelatin mixture. Chill, stirring occasionally, until mixture mounds slightly when dropped from a spoon.

Beat egg whites until soft peaks form; gradually beat in remaining ¼ cup sugar and continue beating until stiff. Fold into gelatin mixture; fold in peaches. Turn into serving glasses or a 5-cup mold. Chill until set.

Yield: 10 ½-cup servings
120 calories per serving

Note: For Peach Cheesecake, double recipe and turn into 9-inch springform pan.

Green Snow

1 envelope unflavored gelatin	¼ cup lime juice
1¼ cups cold water, divided	2 teaspoons grated lime rind
nonnutritive sweetener	2 unbeaten egg whites
equivalent to ¾ cup sugar	green food coloring

Sprinkle gelatin over ½ cup cold water in saucepan. Place over low heat; stir constantly until gelatin dissolves—about 3 minutes. Remove from heat. Stir in nonnutritive sweetener, remaining ¾ cup water, lime juice and rind. Chill until slightly thicker than the consistency of unbeaten egg white. Add unbeaten egg whites and a few drops food coloring. Beat with rotary beater or electric mixer until mixture is fluffy and begins to hold its shape. Turn into a 6-cup mold or bowl; chill until firm. Unmold.

Yield: 6 servings
13 calories per serving

Lemon and Almond Sherbet

2 envelopes unflavored gelatin
3 cups cold water, divided
1/4 teaspoon salt
1 teaspoon grated lemon rind

1/4 cup lemon juice
nonnutritive sweetener
equivalent to 1 cup sugar
1/4 teaspoon almond extract

Sprinkle gelatin over 1 cup cold water in saucepan to soften. Place over low heat and stir constantly until gelatin dissolves—2 or 3 minutes. Remove from heat; stir in remaining 2 cups water, salt, lemon rind and juice, nonnutritive sweetener and almond extract. Pour into 4-cup mold. Chill until firm. Unmold. Garnish with mint leaves.

Yield: 6 servings
12 calories per serving

Raspberry Fluff

3 eggs, separated
1/2 cup skim milk
1 envelope unflavored gelatin
1/2 teaspoon grated lemon rind
1 tablespoon lemon juice

1 cup raspberries, pureed
nonnutritive sweetener
equivalent to 1/4 cup sugar
1/4 teaspoon salt
1/4 cup sugar

Beat together egg yolks and milk. Mix with gelatin in top of double boiler. Place over boiling water; stir constantly until gelatin dissolves and mixture thickens slightly—about 5 minutes. Remove from heat. Stir in lemon rind, lemon juice, raspberry puree, nonnutritive sweetener and salt. Chill, stirring occasionally, until slightly thickened.

Beat egg whites until soft peaks form; gradually add sugar and beat until stiff. Fold into raspberry mixture. Turn into 1-quart bowl and chill until set.

Yield: 6 servings
100 calories per serving

Bazaar Mousse

1 envelope unflavored gelatin	equivalent to 1/2 cup sugar
1/2 cup cold water	2 teaspoons lemon juice
1 pint strawberries, washed and hulled	1/2 teaspoon vanilla
nonnutritive sweetener	1 cup heavy cream, whipped

Sprinkle gelatin over cold water in saucepan. Place over low heat; stir constantly until gelatin dissolves—2 or 3 minutes.

Mash berries, or puree in electric blender. Add to dissolved gelatin with sweetener, lemon juice and vanilla. Chill, stirring occasionally, until mixture mounds slightly when dropped from spoon. Fold in whipped cream. Turn into 3-cup mold or into 6 individual dessert dishes. Chill until firm. Unmold. If desired, garnish with whipped cream and strawberries.

Yield: 6 servings
153 calories per serving

Way-Out Bananas

1 package (10 ounces) frozen strawberries, thawed and drained	1 teaspoon brandy
	2 peaches, halved and pitted, or 4 canned peach halves
2 tablespoons sugar	2 bananas

Place drained strawberries in blender container and puree. Strain to remove seeds; stir in sugar and brandy; chill.

Place a peach half in each of four dessert dishes. Peel bananas, dice them and mound on center of each peach half. Top with strawberry sauce.

Yield: 4 servings
100 calories per serving

Chocolate Chiffon Delight

1 envelope unflavored gelatin	2 eggs, separated
1/4 cup sugar	2 cups skim milk
1/4 cup unsweetened cocoa	1 1/2 teaspoons vanilla
1/8 teaspoon salt	

Mix gelatin, sugar, cocoa and salt in saucepan. Beat egg yolks with milk; stir into gelatin mixture. Place over low heat; stir constantly until gelatin dissolves and mixture thickens slightly—about 5 minutes. Remove from heat; stir in vanilla. Chill, stirring occasionally, until mixture thickens and becomes very lumpy. Turn into large bowl; add unbeaten egg whites. Beat at high speed of electric mixer until double in volume. Turn into individual serving dishes or 1-quart bowl. Chill until set.

Yield: 8 1/2-cup servings
80 calories per serving

Banana-Lime Sherbert

1 envelope unflavored gelatin	1 cup mashed ripe bananas
1/2 cup sugar	(3 medium)
1 2/3 cups nonfat dry milk powder	1 teaspoon lime rind
2 cups cold water	1 tablespoon lime juice

Mix gelatin, sugar and dry milk powder in a medium saucepan. Stir in water. Cook, stirring constantly, over medium heat until gelatin is dissolved—about 5 minutes. Cool; stir in bananas, lime rind and lime juice. Turn into freezer trays or loaf pan. Freeze until firm. Turn into large bowl of electric mixer and beat until smooth. Return to trays and freeze.

Yield: 10 1/2-cup servings
105 calories per serving

Caribbean Banana Treat

1 teaspoon butter or margarine	1/8 teaspoon cinnamon
3 eggs, separated	1 teaspoon grated lime rind
3 tablespoons sugar	3 tablespoons skim milk
3 tablespoons flour	1 1/2 cups diced bananas
1/4 teaspoon baking powder	(3 medium)
1/8 teaspoon salt	

Melt butter in 9-inch skillet that can be placed in oven. Beat egg whites until soft peaks form, beat in sugar and continue beating until stiff peaks form. Beat egg yolks in another small bowl until light and fluffy.

Mix together flour, baking powder, salt, cinnamon and lime rind; stir in milk. Beat milk-and-flour mixture into yolks. Fold yolks into beaten whites; then fold in bananas. Turn into prepared skillet. Bake in 400°F. oven 10 minutes, until puffed and lightly browned.

Yield: 8 servings
100 calories per serving

Almond-Flavored Peach Chiffon Pie

1 envelope unflavored gelatin	1 10-ounce package frozen
4 tablespoons sugar, divided	peach slices, pureed
1/4 teaspoon salt	1/4 teaspoon almond extract
2 eggs, separated	1 teaspoon lemon rind
1/2 cup water	1 tablespoon lemon juice
	6 vanilla wafers

Mix gelatin, 2 tablespoons sugar and salt in top of double boiler. Beat together egg yolks and water; add to gelatin mixture. Place over boiling water and cook, stirring constantly, until gelatin is thoroughly dissolved and mixture thickens slightly—about 5 minutes. Remove from heat; stir in peaches, almond extract, lemon rind and juice. Chill until mixture is slightly thicker than the consistency of unbeaten egg white. Beat with a rotary beater until mixture is light and peaches are blended.

Beat egg whites until stiff, but not dry. Add remaining 2 tablespoons sugar gradually and beat until very stiff. Fold into gelatin mixture.

Stand vanilla wafers around 8-inch pie plate; add peach filling. Chill until set.

Yield: 6 servings
120 calories per serving

Peach Giorgio

1 envelope unflavored gelatin	nonnutritive sweetener
1/4 cup cold water	equivalent to 1/2 cup sugar
1 1/4 cups buttermilk	3/4 teaspoon almond extract
1 tablespoon lemon juice	yellow food coloring
	2 peaches, cut up (1 cup)

Sprinkle gelatin over cold water in saucepan. Place over low heat and stir until gelatin dissolves—about 3 minutes. Remove from heat; add buttermilk, lemon juice, nonnutritive sweetener, almond extract and a few drops yellow food coloring. Chill until mixture is consistency of unbeaten egg white.

Layer gelatin mixture and peaches in 3 parfait glasses, using about 2/3 cup gelatin mixture in each glass. Chill until firm.

Yield: 3 servings
72 calories per serving

Note: For peachy mold, fold peaches into gelatin mixture when it has reached consistency of unbeaten egg white. Turn into 2-cup mold. Chill until firm. Unmold to serve.

Mount Snow Pear

2 cups grated, peeled, firm pears   1/8 teaspoon salt
   (3 medium size)   6 tablespoons sugar, divided
1/4 cup fresh lemon juice   2 egg whites

Mix grated pears, lemon juice, salt and 2 tablespoons sugar.

Beat whites until foamy. Beat in remaining 4 tablespoons sugar gradually and continue beating until stiff. Fold in pear mixture. Spoon into 8 individual dishes. Chill or serve immediately.

Yield: 8 servings
78 calories per serving

CALORIE AND GRAM CHART*

FOOD, AND APPROXIMATE MEASURE	FOOD ENERGY (CALORIES)	PROTEIN (GRAMS)
Apple, raw, 1 medium, 2½" in diam.	76	.4
Apple Betty, 1 cup	344	3.9
Apple butter, 1 tbs.	33	.1
Apple juice, fresh or canned, 1 cup	124	.2
Applesauce, canned unsweetened, 1 cup	100	.5
sweetened, 1 cup	184	.5
Apricots, raw, 3	54	1.1
canned, syrup pack, 4 medium halves, 2 tbs. syrup	97	.7
dried, uncooked, 1 cup (40 small halves)	393	7.8
cooked, unsweetened, 1 cup (25 halves approx.)	242	4.8
cooked, sweetened, 1 cup (25 halves approx.)	400	4.9
frozen, 3 ounces	70	.6
Asparagus, cooked, 1 cup cut spears	36	4.2
canned, green, 1 cup cut spears	38	4.2
Avocado, raw ½ peeled, 3½ × 3/4" diam.	279	1.9
Bacon, crisp, 2 slices	97	4.0
Bananas, raw, 1 large, 8 × 1½"	119	1.6
Barley, pearled, light, dry, 1 cup	708	16.6
Bean sprouts, Chinese, 1 cup	21	2.6
Beans:		
Red kidney, canned or cooked, 1 cup	230	14.6
Other (including navy, pea bean—raw), 1 cup	642	40.7
Baked—pork and molasses, 1 cup	325	15.1
pork and tomato sauce, 1 cup	295	15.1
Beans, lima, immature, cooked, 1 cup	152	8.0
canned, solids and liquid, 1 cup	176	9.5

FOOD, AND APPROXIMATE MEASURE	FOOD ENERGY (CALORIES)	PROTEIN (GRAMS)
Beans, snap:		
green, cooked, 1 cup	27	1.8
canned, drained solids, 1 cup	27	1.8
wax, canned, drained solids, 1 cup	27	1.8
Beef cuts, cooked:		
Chuck, 3 ounces without bone	265	22.0
Flank, 3 ounces without bone	270	21.0
Hamburger, 3 ounces	316	19.0
Porterhouse, 3 ounces without bone	293	20.0
Rib roast, 3 ounces without bone	266	20.0
Round, 3 ounces without bone	197	23.0
Rump, 3 ounces without bone	320	18.0
Sirloin, 3 ounces without bone	257	20.0
Beef, canned:		
Corned beef hash, 3 ounces	120	11.7
Roast beef, 3 ounces	189	21.0
Strained (infant food), 1 ounce	30	4.9
Beef, corned, canned:		
Lean, 3 ounces	159	22.5
Medium fat, 3 ounces	182	21.5
Fat, 3 ounces	221	20.0
Beef, dried or chipped, 1 cup	336	56.6
Beef, dried or chipped, 2 ounces	115	19.4
Beef and vegetable stew, 1 cup	252	12.9
Beer (average 4 pct. alcohol), 8 ounces	114	1.4
Beets, red, raw, 1 cup diced	56	2.1
cooked, 1 cup diced	68	1.6
Beet greens, cooked, 1 cup	39	2.9
Beverages, carbonated:		
Ginger ale, 1 cup	80	—

FOOD, AND APPROXIMATE MEASURE	ENERGY (CALORIES)	PROTEIN (GRAMS)
Beverages, carbonated (cont.):		
Other, including cola type, 1 cup	107	—
Biscuits, baking powder, 1—2½" diam.	129	3.1
Blackberries, raw, 1 cup	82	1.7
canned, syrup pack, 1 cup	216	1.8
Blancmange (vanilla cornstarch puddings), 1 cup	275	8.7
Blueberries, raw, 1 cup	85	.8
canned, syrup pack, 1 cup	245	1.0
frozen without sugar, 3 ounces	52	.5
Bluefish, cooked, baked, 1 piece 3½ × 3 × ½"	193	34.2
fried, 1 piece 3½ × 3 × ½"	307	34.0
Bouillon cubes, 1 cube	2	—
Brains, all kinds, raw, 3 ounces	106	8.8
Bran (breakfast cereal almost wholly bran), 1 cup	145	7.2
Bran flakes, 1 cup	117	4.3
Breads:		
Boston brown, unenriched, 1 slice 3 × ¾"	105	2.3
Cracked-wheat, unenriched, 1 slice ½" thick	60	2.0
French or Vienna, unenriched, 1 pound	1,225	36.8
Italian, unenriched, 1 pound	1,195	39.5
Raisin, unenriched, 1 slice ½" thick	65	1.6
Rye, American, 1 slice ½" thick	57	2.1
White, unenriched, 4 per cent nonfat milk solids, 1 slice ½" thick	63	2.0
Whole wheat, 1 slice ½" thick	55	2.1
Bread crumbs, dry, grated, 1 cup	339	10.5
Broccoli, cooked, 1 cup	44	5.0
Brussels sprouts, cooked, 1 cup	60	5.7
Buckwheat flour:		
Dark, 1 cup sifted	340	11.5

FOOD, AND APPROXIMATE MEASURE	ENERGY (CALORIES)	PROTEIN (GRAMS)
Buckwheat, flour (cont.):		
Light, 1 cup sifted	342	6.3
Buckwheat pancake, 1 cake 4" diam.	47	1.6
Butter, 1 tbs.	100	.1
Buttermilk, 1 cup	86	8.5
Buttermilk, 1 quart	348	34.2
Cabbage, raw, 1 cup shredded fine	24	1.4
cooked, short time, 1 cup	40	2.4
Cabbage, celery or Chinese:		
Raw, leaves and stem, 1 cup 1" pieces	14	1.2
Cooked, 1 cup	27	2.3
Cakes:		
Angel food, 2" sector	108	3.4
Foundation, plain, 1 square 3 × 2 × 1¾"	228	3.8
With fudge icing, 3" sector	314	4.0
Fruit, dark, 1 piece 2 × 2 × ½"	106	1.6
Cupcake, 1, 2¾" in diam.	131	2.6
Iced layer cake, 3" sector	241	3.9
Iced cupcake, 1, 2¾" in diam.	161	2.6
Pound, 1 slice 2¾ × 3 × ⅝"	130	2.1
Rich, 1 square 3 × 2 × 2"	294	3.8
Plain icing, 3" sector	378	4.4
Sponge, 2" sector	117	3.2
Candy:		
Butterscotch, 1 ounce	116	—
Caramels, 1 ounce	118	.8
Chocolate, sweetened milk, 1 ounce	143	2.0
Chocolate creams, 1 ounce	110	1.1
Fondant, 1 ounce	101	—
Fudge, plain, 1 ounce	116	.5
Hard, 1 ounce	108	—

CALORIE AND GRAM CHART (cont.):

FOOD, AND APPROXIMATE MEASURE	FOOD ENERGY (CALORIES)	PROTEIN (GRAMS)
Candy (cont.):		
Marshmallows, 1 ounce	92	.9
Peanut brittle, 1 ounce	125	2.4
Cantaloupe, 1/2 melon 5" diam.	37	1.1
Carrots, raw, 1, 5½ × 1"	21	.6
Grated, 1 cup	45	1.3
Cooked, 1 cup diced	44	.9
Cauliflower, raw, 1 cup flower buds	25	2.4
Cooked, 1 cup	30	2.9
Celery, raw, 1 stalk, 8" long, 1" wide	7	.5
Celery, raw, 1 cup diced	18	1.3
Cooked, 1 cup diced	24	1.7
Chard, cooked, 1 cup	47	4.6
Cheese:		
Camembert, 1 ounce	85	5.0
Cheddar, 1 ounce (1" cube)	113	7.1
Cottage from skim milk, 1 cup	215	43.9
Cottage from skim milk, 2 tbs.	25	6.0
Cream cheese, 1 ounce	106	2.6
Limburger, 1 ounce	97	6.0
Parmesan, 1 ounce	112	10.2
Swiss, 1 ounce	105	7.8
Cherries, raw, sour, sweet, 1 cup pitted	94	1.7
Canned, 1 cup	122	2.0
Chicken, raw, broiler, 1/2 bird (8 ounces bone out)	332	44.4
Roasters, 4 ounces, bone out	227	22.9
Hens, stewing, 4 ounces, bone out	342	20.4
Fryers, 1 breast, 8 ounces, bone out	210	47.0
1 leg, 5 ounces, bone out	159	29.1

FOOD, AND APPROXIMATE MEASURE	FOOD ENERGY (CALORIES)	PROTEIN (GRAMS)
Chili con carne, canned, 1/3 cup (without beans)	170	8.8
Chili sauce, 1 tbs.	17	.5
Chocolate, bitter, 1 ounce	142	1.6
Sweetened, plain, 1 ounce	133	.6
Chocolate beverage, 1 cup (made with milk)	239	8.2
Chocolate syrup, 1 tbs.	42	.2
Cider—See apple juice		
Clams, raw, meat only, 4 ounces	92	14.5
Canned, solids and liquid, 3 ounces	44	6.7
Cocoa, breakfast, plain dry powder, 1 tbs.	21	.6
Cocoa beverage made with all milk, 1 cup	236	9.5
Cola beverage, carbonated, 1 cup	107	—
Coconut, fresh, 1 piece, 2 × 2 × ½"	161	1.5
Dried, shredded, 1 cup	344	2.2
Milk only, 1 cup	60	.7
Cod, raw, 4 ounces edible portion	84	18.7
Dried, 1 ounce	106	23.2
Coffee, clear, 1 cup	—	—
Coleslaw, 1 cup	102	1.6
Collards, cooked, 1 cup	76	7.4
Cookies, plain, 1, 3" diam., ½" thick	109	1.5
Corn, 1 ear 5" long	84	2.7
Canned, solids and liquid, 1 cup	170	5.1
Corn bread or muffins, 1, 2¾" diam.	106	3.2
Corn flakes, 1 cup	96	2.0
Corn flour, 1 cup sifted	406	8.6
Cornmeal (whole) cooked, white or yellow, 1 cup	119	2.6
Corn syrup, 1 tbs.	57	—
Crabs, canned or cooked, 3 oz. (meat only)	89	14.4

FOOD, AND APPROXIMATE MEASURE	ENERGY (CALORIES)	PROTEIN (GRAMS)
Crackers:		
Graham, 4 small	55	1.1
Saltines, 2, 2" square	34	.7
Soda, plain, 2, 2½" square	47	1.1
Cranberries, raw, 1 cup	54	.5
Canned or cooked sauce, 1 cup	549	.3
Cream, light, table, 1 tbs.	30	.4
Heavy, or whipping, 1 tbs.	49	.3
Cress, garden, cooked, 1 cup	73	7.6
Cress, water, raw, 1 pound (leaves & stems)	84	7.7
Cucumbers, raw, 1, 7½ × 2"	25	1.4
Currants, red, raw, 1 cup	60	1.3
Custard, baked, 1 cup	283	13.1
Dandelion greens, 1 cup cooked	79	4.9
Dates, fresh and dried, 1 cup pitted	505	3.9
Doughnuts, cake type, 1	136	2.1
Eggs, boiled, poached, 1	77	6.1
Omelet, 1 egg	106	6.8
Scrambled, 1 egg	106	6.8
Yolk, raw, 1	61	2.8
White, raw, 1	15	3.3
Endive, Escarole, 1 pound raw	90	7.3
Farina, cooked, 1 cup	104	3.1
Fats, cooking (vegetable), 1 tbs.	110	—
See also Lard, Oils		
Figs, raw, 3 small, 1½" diam.	90	1.6
Canned, syrup pack, 3, and 2 tbs. syrup	129	.9

FOOD, AND APPROXIMATE MEASURE	(CALORIES)	(GRAMS)
Figs (cont.):		
Dried, 1 large	57	.8
Fig bars, 1 small	56	.7
Flounder, summer and winter, 4 oz. (raw), edible portion	78	16.9
Frankfurters, 1	124	7.0
Frog legs, raw, 4 oz. edible portion	82	18.6
Fruit cocktail, canned, 1 cup (solids & liquid)	179	1.0
Gelatin, dry, plain, 1 tbs.	34	8.6
Dessert powder, ½ cup (3 ounce pkg.)	324	8.0
Dessert, ready-to-serve, 1 cup	155	3.8
Ginger ale, dry, 1 cup	80	—
Gingerbread, 1 piece 2 × 2 × 2"	180	2.1
Gooseberries, raw, 1 cup	59	1.2
Grapefruit, raw, ½ medium (4½" diam.)	75	.9
Grapefruit, raw, 1 cup sections	77	1.0
Canned in syrup, 1 cup solids & liquid	181	1.5
Juice, fresh, 1 cup	87	1.2
Juice, canned sweetened, 1 cup	131	1.3
Juice, canned unsweetened, 1 cup	92	1.2
Juice, concentrate, frozen, 1 can, 6 fluid ounces	297	3.8
Grapes, raw—Concord, 1 cup skins & seeds	84	1.7
Malaga, Muscat, 1 cup (40 grapes)	102	1.2
Grape juice, bottled, 1 cup	170	1.0
Griddle cakes (wheat), 1 cake, 4" in diam.	59	1.8
Guavas, common, raw, 1	49	.7
Haddock, cooked, 1 fillet 4 × 3 × ½"	158	19.0
Halibut, broiled, 1 steak 4 × 3 × ½"	228	33.0

CALORIE AND GRAM CHART (cont.):

FOOD, AND APPROXIMATE MEASURE	FOOD ENERGY (CALORIES)	PROTEIN (GRAMS)
Ham, See Pork		
Hamburger, See Beef		
Heart, beef, lean, raw, 3 ounces	92	14.4
Chicken, raw, 3 ounces	134	17.4
Herring, smoked, kippered, 3 ounces, edible portion	180	18.9
Hominy grits, cooked, 1 cup	122	2.9
Honey, 1 tbs.	62	.1
Honeydew melon, 1 wedge 2 × 7"	49	.8
Ice cream, plain*, 1/7 of quart brick	167	3.2
* Based on 5 pounds of ice cream to the gallon, factory packed.		
Jams, marmalades, 1 tbs.	55	.1
Jellies, 1 tbs.	50	—
Kale, cooked, 1 cup	45	4.3
Ketchup, tomato, 1 tbs.	17	.3
Kidney, beef, 3 ounces (raw)	120	12.8
Pork, 3 ounces (raw)	97	13.9
Lamb, 3 ounces (raw)	89	14.1
Kohlrabi, raw, 1 cup dried	41	2.9
cooked, 1 cup	47	3.3
Lamb:		
Rib chop cooked, 3 ounces without bone	356	20.0
Shoulder roast, 3 ounces without bone	293	18.0

FOOD, AND APPROXIMATE MEASURE	FOOD ENERGY (CALORIES)	PROTEIN (GRAMS)
Lamb (cont.):		
Leg roast, 3 ounces without bone	230	20.0
Lard, 1 tbs.	126	—
Lemons, 1 medium	20	.6
Juice, fresh, 1 tbs.	4	.1
Lettuce, loose leaf, 1 head	32	2.6
Lettuce, loose leaf, 2 large leaves	7	.6
Limes, 1 medium	19	.4
Juice, fresh, 1 cup	58	1.0
Liver, beef, 2 ounces cooked	118	13.4
Calf, 3 ounces raw	120	16.2
Chicken, 3 ounces raw	120	18.8
Lamb, 3 ounces raw	116	17.8
Liver, canned, strained, 1 ounce (infant food)	30	4.5
Lobster, canned, 3 ounces	78	15.6
Loganberries, raw, 1 cup	90	1.4
Macaroni, enriched, cooked, 1 cup (1" pieces)	209	7.1
Macaroni & cheese baked, 1 cup	464	17.8
Mackerel, canned, 3 ounces solids & liquids	153	17.9
Mangos, raw, 1 medium	87	.9
Margarine, 1 tbs.	101	.1
Marmalade, 1 tbs.	55	.1
Mayonnaise, 1 tbs.	92	.2
Milk, cow: fluid, whole, 1 cup	166	8.5
Fluid, nonfat (skim), 1 cup	87	8.6
Buttermilk, 1 cup	86	8.5
Canned, evaporated (unsweetened), 1 cup	346	17.6

FOOD, AND APPROXIMATE MEASURE	ENERGY (CALORIES)	PROTEIN (GRAMS)
Milk (cont.):		
Condensed (sweetened), 1 cup	981	24.8
Dried, whole, 1 tbs.	39	2.1
Dried, nonfat solids (skim), 1 tbs.	28	2.7
Malted beverage, 1 cup	281	12.4
Half & half (milk and cream), 1 cup	330	7.7
Chocolate flavored, 1 cup	185	8.0
Milk, goat, 1 cup	164	8.1
Molasses, cane, light, 1 tbs.	50	—
Medium, 1 tbs.	46	—
Blackstrap, 1 tbs.	43	—
Barbados, 1 tbs.	54	—
Muffins, plain, 1, 2¾" in diam.	134	3.8
Mung bean sprouts, raw, 1 cup	21	2.6
Mushrooms, canned, 1 cup solids & liquid	28	3.4
Muskmelon, ½ melon 5" diam.	37	1.1
Mustard greens, cooked, 1 cup	31	3.2
Noodles, unenriched, containing		
egg, 1 cup (dry)	278	9.2
Cooked, 1 cup	107	3.5
Nuts:		
Almonds, shelled, 1 cup	848	26.4
Brazil, shelled, 1 cup (32 kernels)	905	20.2
Cashew, roasted, 1 ounce	164	5.2
Peanuts, roasted, 1 cup medium halves	805	38.7
Peanuts, roasted, 1 tbs. chopped	50	2.4
Pecans, 1 cup halves	752	10.2
Pecans, 1 tbs. chopped	52	.7
Walnuts, 1 cup halves	654	15.0
Walnuts, 1 tbs. chopped	49	1.1

FOOD, AND APPROXIMATE MEASURE	ENERGY (CALORIES)	PROTEIN (GRAMS)
Oatmeal or rolled oats, 1 cup dry	312	11.4
Cooked, 1 cup	148	5.4
Oils, salad or cooking, 1 tbs.	124	—
Okra, cooked, 8 pods, 3 × ⅝"	28	1.5
Oleomargarine, 1 tbs.	101	.1
Olives, green, 10 large	72	.8
Ripe, Mission, 10 large	106	1.0
Onions, mature, raw, 1, 2½" diam.	49	1.5
Onions, mature, raw, 1 tbs. chopped	4	.1
Cooked, whole, 1 cup	79	2.1
Onions, young green, 6 small	23	.5
Oranges, 1 medium, 3" diam.	70	1.4
Orange juice, fresh, 1 cup	108	2.0
Canned, unsweetened, 1 cup	109	2.0
Canned, sweetened, 1 cup	135	1.5
Orange juice concentrate, canned, 1 ounce	65	1.2
Frozen, 1 can (6 fl. oz.)	300	5.5
Oysters, meat only, raw, 1 cup (13–19 med.)	200	23.5
Stew, 1 cup (6–8 oysters)	244	16.6
Pancakes (griddle cakes)		
Wheat, 1 cake, 4" diam.	59	1.8
Buckwheat, 1 cake, 4" diam.	47	1.6
Papayas, raw, 1 cup, ½" cubes	71	1.1
Parsley, common, raw, 1 tbs. chopped	1	.1
Parsnips, cooked, 1 cup	94	1.6
Peaches, raw, 1 medium	46	.5
Peaches, canned, syrup pack,		
2 medium halves, 2 tbs. syrup	79	.5
Strained (infant food), 1 ounce	17	.2
Frozen, 4 ounces	89	.5

CALORIE AND GRAM CHART (cont.):

FOOD, AND APPROXIMATE MEASURE	FOOD ENERGY (CALORIES)	PROTEIN (GRAMS)
Peaches (cont.):		
Dried, cooked, no sugar, 1 cup,		
10–12 halves, 6 tbs. liquid	224	2.4
With sugar added, 1 cup,		
10–12 halves, 6 tbs. liquid	366	2.4
Peanut butter, 1 tbs.	92	4.2
Pears, raw, 3 × 2½" diam.	95	1.1
Canned, syrup pack,		
2 medium halves, 2 tbs. syrup	79	.2
Strained (infant food), 1 ounce	15	.2
Peas, green, 1 cup	111	7.8
Canned, 1 cup drained solids	145	7.2
Canned, 1 cup solids & liquid	168	8.5
Peppers, green, raw, 1 medium	16	.8
Persimmons, raw,		
Seedless kind, 1, 2¼" diam.	95	1.0
Kind with seeds, 1, 2¼" diam.	74	.8
Pickles: Dill, 1 large	15	.9
Bread & butter pickles, 6 slices	29	.4
Sour, 1 large	15	.7
Sweet, 1 average	22	.2
Pies: Apple, 4" sector	331	2.8
Blueberry, 4" sector	291	2.8
Cherry, 4" sector	340	3.2
Custard, 4" sector	266	6.8
Lemon meringue, 4" sector	302	4.3
Mince, 4" sector	341	3.4
Pumpkin, 4" sector	263	5.5
Pimientos, canned, 1 medium	10	.3
Pineapple, raw, 1 cup diced	74	.6
Pineapple (cont.):		
Canned, syrup pack, 1 cup crushed	204	1.0
Canned, syrup pack, 1 large slice &		
2 tbs. juice	95	.5
Frozen, 4 ounces	97	.5
Pineapple juice, canned, 1 cup	121	.7
Plums, raw, 1, 2" in diam.	29	.4
Canned, syrup pack, 1 cup (fruit & juice)	186	1.0
Popcorn, popped, 1 cup	54	1.8
Pork, fresh:		
Ham cooked, 3 ounces without bone	338	20.0
Loin or chops cooked, 1 chop	293	20.0
Pork, cured:		
Ham, smoked, cooked, 3 ounces without bone	339	20.0
Luncheon meat: Boiled ham, 2 ounces	172	12.9
Canned, spiced, 2 ounces	164	8.4
Pork sausage, links, raw, 4 ounces	510	12.2
Pork, canned, strained, 1 ounce (infant food)	36	4.8
Potatoes, baked, 1 medium, 2½" diam.	97	2.4
Boiled in jacket, 1 medium, 2½" diam.	118	2.8
Peeled and boiled, 1 medium, 2½" diam.	105	2.5
French-fried, 8 pieces 2 × ½ × ½"	157	2.2
Hashed-brown, 1 cup	470	6.4
Mashed, milk added, 1 cup	159	4.3
Mashed, milk and butter added, 1 cup	240	4.1
Steamed or pressure cooked, 1 medium	105	2.5
Canned, drained solids, 3–4 very small	118	2.8
Potato chips, 10 medium, 2" diam.	108	1.3
Pretzels, 5 small sticks	18	.04
Prunes, dried, uncooked, 4 large	94	.8

FOOD, AND APPROXIMATE MEASURE	ENERGY (CALORIES)	PROTEIN (GRAMS)
Prunes (cont.):		
Cooked, no sugar added, 1 cup	310	2.7
Cooked, sugar added, 1 cup	483	2.9
Prunes, canned, strained,		
1 ounce (infant food)	28	.3
Prune juice, canned, 1 cup	170	1.0
Prune whip, 1 cup	200	3.8
Pudding, vanilla, 1 cup	275	8.7
Puffed rice, 1 cup	55	.8
Puffed wheat, 1 cup	43	1.3
Pumpkin, canned, 1 cup	76	2.3
Radishes, raw, 4 small	4	.2
Raisins, dried, 1 cup	429	3.7
Raisins, dried, 1 tbs.	26	.2
Cooked, sugar added, 1 cup	572	3.2
Raspberries, black, raw, 1 cup	100	2.0
Red, raw, 1 cup	70	1.5
Frozen, 3 ounces	84	.7
Rhubarb, raw, 1 cup diced	19	.6
Cooked, sugar added, 1 cup	383	1.1
Rice, brown, raw, 1 cup	784	15.6
Cooked, 1 cup	204	4.2
White, raw, 1 cup	692	14.5
White, cooked, 1 cup	201	4.2
White, precooked, dry, 1 cup	420	9.7
Wild rice, parched, raw, 1 cup	593	23.0
Rice, flakes, 1 cup	118	1.8
Rolls, plain, pan rolls, unenriched		
(12 per pound), 1	118	3.4
Sweet, unenriched, 1	178	4.8

FOOD, AND APPROXIMATE MEASURE	ENERGY (CALORIES)	PROTEIN (GRAMS)
Rutabagas, cooked, 1 cup cubed or sliced	50	1.2
Rye flour, light, 1 cup sifted	285	7.5
Rye wafers, 2	43	1.6
Salad dressings:		
Commercial, plain (mayonnaise type), 1 tbs.	58	.2
French, 1 tbs.	59	.1
Mayonnaise, 1 tbs.	92	.2
Salad oil, 1 tbs.	124	—
Salmon, broiled, baked, 1 steak 4 × 3 × ½"	204	33.6
Canned, solids and liquid:		
Chinook or king, 3 ounces	173	16.8
Chum, 3 ounces	118	18.3
Coho or silver, 3 ounces	140	17.9
Pink or humpback, 3 ounces	122	17.4
Sockeye or red, 3 ounces	147	17.2
Sardines: Atlantic type, canned in oil:		
Solids and liquid, 3 ounces	288	17.9
Drained solids, 3 ounces	182	21.9
Pilchards, Pacific type:		
Canned, solids and liquid		
Natural pack, 3 ounces	171	15.1
Tomato sauce, 3 ounces	184	15.1
Sauerkraut, canned, 1 cup drained solids	32	2.1
Sausage: Bologna, 1 piece 1 × 1½" diam.	467	31.2
Frankfurter, cooked, 1	124	7.0
Liver, liverwurst, 2 ounces	150	9.5
Pork, links or bulk, 4 ounces (raw)	510	12.2
Vienna, canned, 4 ounces	244	17.9
Scallops, raw, 4 ounces edible muscle	89	16.8
Shad, raw, 4 ounces edible portion	191	21.2

CALORIE AND GRAM CHART (cont.):

FOOD, AND APPROXIMATE MEASURE	FOOD ENERGY (CALORIES)	PROTEIN (GRAMS)
Sherbet, ½ cup	118	1.4
Shortbread, 2 squares, 1¾ × 1¾"	81	1.1
Shredded wheat, 1 large biscuit, plain	102	2.9
Shrimp, canned, 3 ounces drained solids	110	23.0
Syrup, table blends (chiefly corn syrup), 1 tbs.	57	—
Soups, canned:		
Bean, ready-to-serve, 1 cup	191	8.5
Beef, ready-to-serve, 1 cup	100	6.0
Bouillon, broth, and consommé, ready-to-serve, 1 cup	9	2.0
Chicken, ready-to-serve, 1 cup	75	3.5
Clam chowder, ready-to-serve, 1 cup	86	4.6
Cream soup—asparagus, celery, mushroom, 1 cup	201	7.0
Noodle, rice or barley, 1 cup	117	6.0
Pea, ready-to-serve, 1 cup	141	6.4
Tomato, ready-to-serve, 1 cup	90	2.2
Vegetable, ready-to-serve, 1 cup	82	4.2
Vegetable, strained, 1 ounce (infant food)	12	.7
Soybeans, whole, mature, dried, 1 cup	695	73.3
Soybean flour, 1 cup stirred	232	37.4
Soybean sprouts, raw, 1 cup	49	6.6
Spaghetti, dry, unenriched, 1 cup 2" pieces	354	12.0
Cooked, 1 cup	218	7.4
Spinach, raw, 4 ounces edible portion	22	2.6
Cooked, 1 cup	46	5.6
Strained (infant food), 1 ounce	4	.5
Squash, summer, cooked, 1 cup diced	34	1.3
Winter, baked, mashed, 1 cup	97	3.9

FOOD, AND APPROXIMATE MEASURE	FOOD ENERGY (CALORIES)	PROTEIN (GRAMS)
Squash (cont.):		
Winter, canned, strained, 1 ounce (infant food)	8	.3
Starch, pure (corn), 1 tbs.	29	—
Strawberries, raw, 1 cup capped	54	1.2
Frozen, 3 ounces	90	.5
Sugars:		
Granulated, cane or beet, 1 cup	770	—
1 teaspoon	16	—
1 lump 1⅛ × ⅝ × ⅛"	27	—
Powdered, 1 cup (stirred before measuring)	493	—
1 tbs.	31	—
Brown, 1 cup (firm-packed)	813	—
1 tbs.	51	—
Maple, 1 piece 1¾ × 1¼ × ½"	104	—
Sweet potatoes, baked, 1, 5 × 2"	183	2.6
Boiled, 1, 5 × 2½"	252	3.7
Candied, 1 small	314	2.6
Canned, 1 cup	233	4.4
Swordfish, broiled, 1 steak 3 × 3 × ½"	223	34.2
Tangerine, 1 medium	35	.6
Juice, unsweetened, 1 cup	95	2.2
Tapioca, dry granulated quick-cooking, stirred, 1 cup	547	.9
Tomatoes, raw, 1 medium, 2 × 2½"	30	1.5
Canned or cooked, 1 cup	46	2.4
Juice, canned, 1 cup	50	2.4
Tomato ketchup, 1 tbs.	17	.3

FOOD, AND APPROXIMATE MEASURE	FOOD ENERGY (CALORIES)	PROTEIN (GRAMS)
Tomato puree, canned, 1 cup	90	4.5
Tongue, beef, medium fat, raw, 4 ounces	235	18.6
Tortillas, 1, 5" diam.	50	1.2
Tuna fish, canned, 3 oz. solids & liquid	247	20.2
Tuna fish, canned, 3 oz. drained solids	169	24.7
Turkey, medium fat, raw, 4 oz. edible portion	304	22.8
Turnips, raw, 1 cup diced	43	1.5
Cooked, 1 cup diced	42	1.2
Turnip greens, cooked, 1 cup	43	4.2
Veal, cooked, cutlet, 3 ounces without bone	184	24.0
Shoulder roast, 3 ounces without bone	193	24.0
Stew meat, 3 ounces without bone	252	21.0
Veal, canned, strained, 1 ounce (infant food)	24	4.5
Vinegar, 1 tbs.	2	—
Waffles, 1	216	7.0
Watercress, raw, 1 pound (leaves & stems)	84	7.7
Watermelon, ½ slice ¾ × 10"	45	.8
Wheat flour, whole, 1 cup stirred	400	16.0
Wheat products:		
Breakfast flakes, 1 cup	125	3.8
Puffed, 1 cup	43	1.0
Rolled, cooked, 1 cup	177	5.0
Shredded, plain, 1 small biscuit 2½ × 2"	79	2.0
Whole meal, cooked, 1 cup	175	6.6
Wheat germ, 1 cup stirred	246	17.1
White sauce, medium, 1 cup	429	10.0
Wild rice, parched, raw, 1 cup	593	23.0
Yeast, dried, brewer's, 1 tbs.	22	3.0
Yogurt, commercial made with whole milk, 1 cup	170	11.0

Calorie Content of Alcoholic Beverages

DRINK	QUANTITY (OUNCES)	CALORIES
Beer	12	150
Rum	1½	150
Whiskey	1½	110
Grasshopper	2	200
Manhattan	2	140
Martini	2	160
Old-fashioned	2	170
Whiskey sour	2	140
Liqueur	1	100
Wine, dry, 20%	4	160
Wine, light dry, 12%	4	100
Wine, sweet, 20%	4	180

CHAPTER 4

Body-Shaping Clothes

After many years of being photographed in fabulous furs, gowns and jewels, I might, if I had my way, have only two large-size sweatshirts, two pairs of blue jeans and a pair of sneakers in my personal wardrobe. But it is hardly practical for a woman who, like me, is both a wife and mother and a career woman to even consider such a solution to the problem of what to wear. It's only a dream, and a pretty silly one at that. Perhaps silly isn't the right word, so I'll substitute rebellious and adolescent. There is a time and place for everything, and going to a football game in a cocktail dress would be just as ridiculous as appearing at the opera in stadium boots.

Understand that I don't mean we should all be cut from the same bolt of lace. When pantsuits were first shown in the leading fashion magazines, I was one of the first to wear one to the Royal Ballet opening at the Metropolitan. I knew I was being stared at by some of the older patrons, and even though I was confident that I was dressed in good taste, I felt slightly offbeat. My fears were dissipated during intermission when several ladies approached to ask where they could order similar outfits.

On the other hand, to please my husband, I wore the same ensemble to a prominent New York City restaurant and we were refused entry. Setting fashion trends takes courage.

Many of today's successful models feel as I do about clothes. Often they make rounds in informal attire. Unlikely as it might seem, working in beautiful clothes day in and day out can lead to a bit of boredom, and a model likes to keep a fresh approach to fashion. When a busy model leaves her apartment in the morning, she knows exactly where she will be almost from minute to minute. She knows that she'll be seen only by the photographers with whom she works and the taxi drivers who carry her from job to job. It is surprising how quickly a model adapts to doing everything from making up to repairing a broken fingernail in the back of a jouncing cab.

For anyone other than the most established model, however, it must always be best foot forward—the look of today, not yesterday, with perhaps a touch of tomorrow. Clothes need not be expensive, but they should be "now." One of the nice things about the current fashions is that they do not have to be costly.

As I look back on my early days in modeling, I realize that I was more fortunate than many of my colleagues, for my mother was, and still is, a magical seamstress who can whip out a finished dress in a matter of a couple of hours. When I began working, it was usually something I designed or copied from a fashion magazine. When an emergency arose for an outfit I needed but couldn't borrow or buy, we would work far into the early hours of the morning. Together we always managed to produce whatever the client demanded. I think my having a reputation for being able to come up with the right clothes at the right time had a great deal to do with my rapid success. When I left Chicago for Paris I had about everything a model could possibly dream of having in her wardrobe, and almost all of it was homemade.

If you are thinking of improving your fashion image on a budget, I strongly advise you to take up sewing, choosing your fabrics wisely to approximate those used in the great designer collections.

In planning your wardrobe, try to keep its elements extremely simple. A black, brown, navy blue or gray dress can, when properly accessorized, serve many purposes and create an untold number of illusions. A pin, a scarf, a belt can work miracles. Even if you have scads of money, don't try to buy a complete wardrobe all at once. Take your time, and plan. Impulsive buying most often leads to negative results.

Time after time I have asked my models how they developed a sense of style. The answer is invariably that they started as teen-agers looking at fashion magazines and dreamed of the day when they could wear beautiful clothes. They were developing individuality through the years. However, individuality without taste can become fashion chaos. "Do your own thing" is a principle with which I am in full accord, but one must acquire some background before a sense of style can be achieved. So—one simple rule: stay aware of what's current in fashion. Buy magazines that cater to your age and type. Study the trends closely. Don't be afraid to try something new just because you are comfortable in what you've been wearing. Be slightly daring and sometimes even avant-garde, for that's what it's all about; but in making your selections, always take your own special figure problems into consideration. There are some shapes that just can't be dieted or exercised away—they're a matter of genes. But with a little know-how, it's possible to camouflage just about any contour problem you have. In fact, even if you don't have any glaring figure faults, it's a good idea to understand what clothes can do: that snug ribbing can play up good proportions but accent bad ones; that hip-hugging pants can minimize a droopy behind; that horizontal stripes make any figure seem shorter and fatter. A couple of basic ideas: Don't squeeze into a tight-fitting garment just to say you wear a size 7; you'll only call attention to the problem. A lumpy size 7 is far inferior to a smooth, sleek-looking size 9. On the other hand, don't hide your figure under a tentlike shape. You're only admitting that a problem exists and you don't know how to handle it. Your solution lies in recognizing your problem areas and finding the clothes that disguise them as well as possible. That's what models do when they want to look as good off-camera as they do on. Here's a rundown on how they handle problems:

BROAD SHOULDERS

Steer clear of padding, puffed sleeves or large, broad collars. Also, no halter dresses or deep scoop necklines. Simple high necklines or Vs are fine for you.

SMALL ROUNDED SHOULDERS

You'll look your best in long-sleeved or sleeveless dresses—they won't cut your shoulder proportions. Don't buy anything with a lot of fuss around the neck, either—drawstrings, lace, gathering, etc. Stay away from fussy short sleeves, too; they'll clutter up your own sleek though small lines.

THIN NARROW SHOULDERS

Big puffy sleeves are wrong for you too—they'll drown your proportions.

Stay away from skinny ribbing or absolutely clinging knits too—they'll show you up to be a skeleton. Take advantage of some of the luscious heavier fabrics—wools, tweeds, linen and others—to fill you out.

BIG BOSOM

Don't exaggerate your figure by wearing supertight tops, cinching your waist wasp-thin or wearing Empire lines. Your good shape will show through loose, gently flowing clothes to its best advantage.

FLAT BOSOM

With today's fashions, you're hardly at a disadvantage unless you're just about bosomless. But even if you are, don't try to add heavy padding —it's usually too obvious. Rather, try a soft, fiber-filled padded bra with rounded, natural lines if you really want more of a shape. If not, take advantage of the snug body-fitting clothes that are such great fashion now.

THICK MIDRIFF AND WAIST

Don't try to cinch in your waist—you'll only draw attention to its size. Rather, stick to slightly fitted A-line dresses; long blousy waists; long sweaters, jackets and tunics.

SKINNY MIDRIFF

This isn't a real problem; at least, it's a feature most girls envy. But if you really think it looks bad, treat it the same way you'd treat the thick midriff and waist, above.

BIG HIPS AND BUTTOCKS

Long sweaters, tunics and jackets can be your biggest help if you wear them just the right length—not too short, but not so long that they cut your height to make you look dumpy. Don't cinch your waist—that will exaggerate the size below; stick to A-lines, pleats or the softest, slightest gathers.

NO HIPS

Take fullest advantage of curves: cinch your waist; wear full gathers and pleats. You can also wear thick, nubbly materials that someone with the opposite problem couldn't.

HEAVY LEGS AND THIGHS

For heavy thighs, follow the same rules as for big hips: long jackets, tunics and sweaters if they aren't too hip-hugging. For heavy calves, wear dark-colored stockings—sheer or opaque—but stay away from heavy textures. No skinny heels, either—they will look out of proportion with the bulk of your legs.

SKINNY LEGS

Don't wear skirts so full that your legs look like toothpicks. And if you like below-the-knee skirts, choose the exact length carefully. There's no formula for getting the skirt to the right length—that's for your eye to determine—but if it doesn't hit your leg at the right place, you'll look dowdy rather than chic. Also consider pants and heavy textured stockings —they're great camouflages.

These tricks deal with hiding your faults. But one of the best ways to detract from them is to play up your good features. If you have beautiful legs, show them off; if you have a perfect bustline, wear clothes that play it up—clingy knits and plunging necklines. Beautiful hair and a pretty face always get second glances.

Above all, if you're hiding something, don't ruin the effect by confessing to the whole world that you're buxom or flat-chested. You know your own figure failures better than anyone else. You've been studying them in the most minute detail. But you're the only one who has to know. Choose clothes that compliment your figure; don't announce your defects and no one will be any the wiser. Instead of your being a slave to fashion that doesn't suit your body, fashion will be the handmaiden that serves your own very positive approach to style and beauty in body-shaping clothes selected with forethought and taste.

CHAPTER 5

Model-Tested Skin Care

Part of the "model myth" is that we all have lovely peaches-and-cream complexions while all other women struggle with problem skin. Certainly we work at having good complexions, because we know that much of our success depends upon the condition of our skin. We learn not to take beautiful skin for granted.

Since my teens I've had a running battle with blemishes. As a result, I'm fanatical about skin care, because no matter how much attention I've given my skin, I've still had several very serious bouts with infection and found myself racing to the dermatologist.

Once the photographer, the beauty editor for a leading fashion magazine and I attempted to find a new and exciting "space age" look. We experimented with all types of makeup. Finally we decided on an aura of gold or bronze. We combined actual metallic powder with makeup base and put a thick layer of the mixture on my face. After working all day and into the night, the editor and photographer were satisfied that we had obtained the desired effect. I did a hurried makeup removal and headed for home. Too tired to follow my regular program of skin care, I gave my face a quick wash with soap and warm water, patted on some astringent, grabbed my pot of hot soup and headed for what I consider to be one of life's great luxuries: eating in bed while watching television. Two days later I paid the price for my self-indulgence. Some of the metal particles had lodged in my pores, causing a serious infection. Had I steamed my face and observed my normal routine, I am quite sure the pain and inconvenience I suffered could have been avoided. As it turned out, I was unable to work for two weeks, I spent a great deal of money to restabilize my complexion and what is worse, I still have to cope with two enlarged pores, one on my left cheek and one on my right, as souvenirs of stupid laziness.

Your skin is you. You can't crawl out of it, so you are well advised to live within it graciously. Although you cover most of it with clothing for reasons of fashion, protection and warmth, what you do with the portion that remains uncovered determines the initial impression of your beauty in the eyes of an observing world. Clean, healthy skin is the cornerstone of good looks. Unfortunately, a lovely freshness can't be achieved without effort and understanding.

Skin blemishes are due to a variety of difficulties. For the average person, dirty pores clogged by the natural body oil are one of the biggest offenders. Simple changes in weather can play havoc. All the makeup in the world can't patch up a poor complexion—drab, flaked skin or patches of pimples. A lively, clear complexion is something a model—or anyone—can have with the right know-how.

Diet is step one of the beauty plan. It's impossible to have a soft, radiant complexion without a plentiful supply of the A and B vitamins you read about in Chapter 3. Leave gooey, oily foods, soft drinks and pastries off your food list and seek nutrition. But remember that eating all the right foods in the world isn't sufficient unless your skin gets pamper-special care too.

FACE PAMPERING

A model must determine her skin type; so must we all. Most charts show four basic skin types—normal, dry, oily and combination.

Dry skin is a result of the fact that oil glands beneath the surface do not supply enough moisturizing lubrication. This tends to create a skin that wrinkles and lines more quickly than other skin types. Dry skin needs the gentlest care and added lubricants day and night.

Oily skin is caused by the opposite glandular action. Excess oil blocks the pores and oxidizes to cause blackheads, whiteheads or skin eruptions. Keep an oily skin scrupulously clean at all times by frequent cleansing.

Combination skin is just that. Usually cheeks, eyes and jaw areas possess dry skin while the forehead, nose and chin are too oily. Combination treatment is necessary to keep this kind of skin well balanced.

BASIC SKIN CARE

No matter what type of skin you have, skin care takes time. Allow yourself plenty of leisure in your beauty schedule for thorough face washing morning and night. Start by binding your hair back, or sleek it away from your face with a headband. Then you'll be able to lather clear to the hairline, where makeup has a tendency to collect.

NIGHT

The evening skin ritual starts with cleansing cream or lotion to remove makeup and collected grime. Smooth it all over your skin; then remove it gently with facial tissue. Be careful not to rub or pull your skin—rough treatment is injurious to any skin type. A facial sauna is a good idea once a week or more (depending on your skin) to open and gently flush the pores. Though there are now several facial saunas on the market you can buy, there's one that hardly costs a penny. Just fill a bowl or sink with boiling water, drape a terry towel over your head and soak up the steam for about five minutes. Then, whether you've saunaed or not, make mounds of rich lather with a mild soap and wash with a gentle circular motion, being especially careful around the eye area. Rinse and splash with cool water to close pores again, then pat dry. Finally, apply moisturizer. This goes for oily skin too. A lot of women mistake oil for moisture and end up with overoily yet moisture-starved skin.

MORNING

In the course of a night's sleep, skin secretions build up, so wash your face gently with a mild soap once again. Rinse it with cool water and pat dry. Always follow with moisturizer—and makeup if you wish.

SPECIAL SKIN CARE

This section applies to just about everyone, since each of us has a few special skin requirements. No complexion can be fresh and healthy and stay young-looking as long as possible without the attention it needs.

DRY SKIN

Most young women look forward to the time when oil glands secrete less so that they will no longer have to cope with blemishes and a shiny face. But many permit their skin to go straight from shiny to dry and taut without knowing how to establish an equilibrium. Others who never experience skin problems consider themselves lucky in adolescence because they don't have to do much for a pretty complexion. They, however, are prime targets for premature wrinkling unless they start to pamper their skins at the very beginning. Pampering means special gentleness. To remove makeup, use a superrich cleansing cream or lotion. Most cosmetic brands have a cleanser designed for dry skin; ask your saleswoman for help in choosing the one best for you. Wash your skin with *warm* water—hot water will dry your skin to an even greater degree. Use a mild soap—maybe one of the superfatted soaps available in your drugstore—and lather up gently with the tips of your fingers instead of a facecloth. Then rinse with *cool* water—even cold water is too harsh for dry skin—and gently pat dry. Whether you put makeup on right away or not, be sure to cover your skin with a generous slick of moisturizer immediately. After cleansing at bedtime, use a special night cream on your face, and concentrate it around the eye area. Don't neglect your neck; so many women do, and it's usually the first place upon which signs of age become apparent.

Because the pores of a dry skin collect impurities too, it's smart to treat yourself to a facial sauna once a week. Smooth a rich cream on your face and throat before steaming. After the sauna treatment, splash your face with cool water, gently pat dry and apply moisturizer immediately.

As an extra, treat your skin to a honey-and-egg mask while you relax. It's a stimulating pickup for dry skin, inexpensive and simple to prepare. Just beat a tablespoon of pure, strained honey and one egg yolk together. Smooth on your face and neck, lie down on your bed or in a reclining chair and relax for fifteen minutes. Remove the mask with a towel dipped in lukewarm water.

When applying cosmetics, steer clear of cake makeup and lots of powdering; both will tend to accentuate even the smallest lines. Choose a creamy foundation and blusher, and be especially careful to dust away any excess powder after you've set your makeup.

OILY SKIN

A rich diet is oily skin's worst enemy. Soap and water are its best friends. The tricks in caring for oily skin are to stay away from fried or creamed foods that stimulate already hyperactive oil production and to wash your face often—six or eight times a day if necessary—to keep your skin immaculately clean. Before washing, remove your makeup with a nongreasy cleanser. When you wash, use a medicated soap—one that will control the bacterial growth which causes blemishes. Use a nubby washcloth, but be gentle. Cleanse in a light circular motion instead of rubbing— which irritates the skin and stimulates the oil glands to work double duty. Some doctors recommend washing for as long as three to five minutes to deep-clean pores and stir up circulation; check your own physician on this method. After washing, rinse with cold water—about twenty splashes—to close your pores; then gently pat dry. Even though you think your skin has all the lubrication it needs, use a light moisturizing lotion day and night. Oil and moisture aren't the same thing.

Sauna steaming is an important part of your skin ritual: the warm vapor opens the pores, penetrates and gently flushes out the blocked oil. This prevents formation of blackheads or pimples. Before you start, lather with medicated soap and let the lather dry on your face. Then you're ready to steam; five minutes should do it. Follow up with cold splashes, then moisturizer. Perform this ritual three times a week or, if you find it necessary, more.

A special facial mask can do wonders to stimulate circulation too. Make a paste of dry oatmeal and warm water. Smooth it on, let it dry, then rinse it off with cold water. You can practically feel a healthy pink glow coming to your cheeks.

A rule for blackheads or pimples common to oily skin is *Keep hands off!* If you must break that rule for any reason, follow these instructions for removal without risking infection or scarring. Steam your face for about five minutes. Then cover your fingers with tissue and press gently. If blackheads don't pop out immediately, don't force. Wait for a day, then try once more. For pimples topped with a whitehead, sterilize a needle, puncture the pimple, gently squeeze, then dot with alcohol. Don't tamper with pimples that haven't come to the whitehead stage; you're likely to infect them.

Many cosmetics are manufactured specially for oily skin—some of them medicated. Find one that's good for you and stick to it, but be very careful around your eyes. Avoid using products that may cause drying in that area. To blot makeup between cleansings, try the paper facial blotters made specially for that purpose. They keep your skin shine-free without the necessity of adding layer after layer of powder to your skin.

COMBINATION SKIN

This dual skin type needs two kinds of treatment—dry-skin care around your eyes, cheeks, throat and jaw and oily-skin care on your forehead, nose and chin. You may have to experiment to reach a happy medium, but beautiful skin is worth the time.

The question of a facial mole is a matter of attitude. Some people consider moles to be beauty marks and accentuate them, while others prefer to cover them with makeup or have them removed. Never, absolutely never, try to remove a mole yourself. It is exceedingly dangerous. An undesired skin blemish should always be removed by a physician. Most such operations are simple, inexpensive and seldom uncomfortable.

In cases of skin trouble due to allergies, seek professional help from a dermatologist as quickly as possible. It's his job to give you the proper treatment. Don't take any chance using home remedies that might mar your skin forever.

If we agree that individuality is what counts most in the search for the best results, perhaps you'd like to take a clue from my personal system of daily complexion care. These guidelines can help you establish your own personal skin routine.

In the morning, after having my orange juice and tea, I shower and begin my premakeup facial. Using warm running water, I soak my face in my cupped hands for four or five rinses. I apply a mild soap, one that has proved acceptable for my particular skin, to a freshly laundered washcloth (never one that has been used and then hung up to dry, for it can be filled with germs). I pass the washcloth gently but thoroughly over my face. Then with my cupped hands, still using warm water, I completely rinse and rerinse until I am sure all traces of soap have been removed. Next I gradually lower the temperature of the water to cool and continue rinsing to give my pores a chance to close. I blot my face dry with a freshly laundered towel and gently pat my face with a cotton ball saturated with medicated astringent. After allowing the astringent to dry, I apply a moisturizing lotion all over my face. It acts as a protective layer between the makeup and my skin. After my face is refreshed and dry, I begin the makeup program you'll read about in Chapter 8.

When I arrive home in the evening (even if I am going out again later), I immediately remove my makeup so that my skin can breathe, if only for a few minutes. First I take off my eye makeup with a special eye-cosmetic-remover pad. Then I follow with a special cleansing lotion which I apply in small circular upward movements. When my makeup is removed, I go through the process once again just to make sure. I use the same face-washing procedure I followed in the morning, all the way through to the astringent. If I'm preparing for bed, I apply night cream sparingly around my eyes and other dry areas of my face. About twice a week I use a facial sauna before applying the night cream.

Once a week, I use a mask immediately after my facial sauna. After the sauna my pores are wide open, and the mask gives them the deep cleaning they seem to require. Then I follow with a warm-to-cool rinse and the usual astringent and night cream.

There are conflicting theories on whether or not soap and water is beneficial. I know certain beauty authorities who would never consider doing as I do. They adhere to a skin-care philosophy that includes the use of creams, oils and lotions only. Maybe it's psychological, but if I omit this phase of my beauty care. I don't feel fresh enough.

One extremely important point: I never use extremes of water temperature on my face. Water that is too hot or too cold can and does cause disruptions of tiny facial blood vessels that leave permanent red blemishes in their wake—something that is to be avoided at all costs.

FACIAL EXERCISES

Your face muscles need exercise just as the other parts of your body do. These muscle toners keep your skin from drooping and sagging or maybe even looking just plain tired. Here are a few I do when I'm reading, or watching television or anytime I'm alone. You can do them too.

1. Open your mouth as wide as you can and make your face seem as long as possible; then close your mouth and eyes tightly and try to squeeze your face as small as you can.

2. Roll your head around in a full circle. You can feel chin muscles stretch as you go.

3. Open your mouth wide, hold it open with your fingers pulling down on your bottom teeth and try to close your mouth against the pressure.

4. Chew gum vigorously for about five minutes.

5. Stick your tongue out as far as possible, trying to touch the tip of your nose.

6. Puff out your cheeks; then roll the air around your mouth, forcing it first to the right cheek, then to the left and finally to the front of your mouth.

I do these exercises every day as many times as possible. There's no guarantee of a lifetime of wrinkle-free skin, but I'm convinced these exercises help.

ENEMIES OF SKIN BEAUTY

Most dermatologists agree that overexposure to the sun is the main cause of prematurely aging skin. Though a burnished brown tan may be beautiful for a few weeks, it takes years off your skin's life. A light golden tan that develops slowly is a beautiful way for skin to have a healthy outdoor glow, yet stay smooth and soft later. This means limiting sunbathing, especially in the beginning. Apply a generous slick of suntan lotion, or a sun screen if your skin has even the slightest tendency to burn. Cover your lips with lots of lip gloss. A broad-brimmed hat and sunglasses are good ideas too—they help keep squint lines away. In fact, some models alternate two pairs of sunglasses, differently shaped—switching off to avoid an owl-eye effect.

Lack of sleep is another skin ager. If models are the most gorgeous girls around, it's because you'll rarely see them out and around the town night after night. Sleep is part of the beauty life. They can't skimp on rest without looking the worse for it. Not everyone needs exactly eight hours a night: some need more, some less. A glance at the mirror in the morning can usually tell you if you've had enough sleep.

Liquor, because it dehydrates the skin and enlarges pores, is another skin ager. This isn't to say that one must cut out all liquor to have beautiful skin, but in excess, alcoholic beverages are one of the worst things for the complexion.

Nothing pinches and tightens your looks more than tension. Knowing how to relax is one of the biggest aids to beauty. In the high-pressure world of fashion, models have to know how to deal with tension quickly. Different women handle it differently. Just about everyone agrees that a soothing bath, chin-deep in bubbles, is one of the best methods. A hand-sized vibrating massager is effective too; it's good not only for muscle relaxing, but also in stimulating circulation for healthy skin and hair.

BODY PAMPERING

Complexion doesn't stop at your head; it goes all the way down to your toes, and every inch needs the same special care you give your face. Work it into your daily bath or shower ritual. Start with a brisk rubdown. Use a rough dry towel all over your body. This revs up sluggish circulation. Then smooth bath oil all over your body—instead of putting it into the tub. This gives it a chance to soak into your skin. Wrap yourself in a towel and relax while your bath is filling (or for about five minutes if you're taking a shower). Luxuriate in your bath or shower; and unless it's just before bedtime, rub briskly with a washcloth to stimulate allover circulation. After your bath, lubricate all over with lotion—a hand lotion is as good as anything—then dust lightly with a prettily scented talcum powder.

Some women prefer to defuzz their legs and underarms at bath time; others don't. Very often it depends on the method used. Most models use a cream depilatory; its results are longer-lasting than shaving, and you don't run the risk of cutting or scratching your legs. It's best to use depilatory cream just before bath or shower. Smooth on the cream, wait the prescribed time and the hair will wash away.

Fewer models shave their legs and underarms. Of the two shaving methods, a hand razor gives a closer shave than an electric razor, but even so, the hair comes back more rapidly in a prickly stubble, and often they have to shave every day to stay as smooth as necessary for their work. Shaving that often is hard on the skin.

Electrolysis and waxing are two less commonly used methods for getting rid of excess hair. Electrolysis is permanent. It is usually used only for small areas such as the upper lip or chin, as it must be done by a licensed professional and is very expensive. It would literally cost a fortune to do the legs. Waxing is less expensive—in fact, it costs very, very little if you learn how to do it yourself—but the hair has to reach an unattractive length before it can be removed. Aside from that, it's painful. When the hardened wax is pulled off, the hair comes along in about the same way it would with adhesive tape. It feels about the same way, too.

Pamper-perfect care means proper, consistent attention to the skin on every part of your body, using every modern cosmetic designed for that purpose.

It means scrupulous cleanliness.

It means protecting that skin from overexposure to wind, weather and the pollution of our atmosphere.

Pamper-perfect care means a more beautiful, "touchable" you from head to toe.

CHAPTER 6

Beautiful Hands and Feet

Whether or not we are aware of it, each of us develops a barometer by which she makes instant appraisals of other people. One I use, which is extremely accurate, is the condition of a model's hands, especially her fingernails. It is one of the first things I look for when a potential model is brought into my office. No matter what illusion she may otherwise create, the state of her hands and nails tells me whether she cares enough about her appearance to be a professional.

A complete manicure at least once a week should be part of your body pampering, no matter how busy your schedule. You can be the most beautiful person in the world, but if your hands aren't well groomed, your beauty is sullied. Your hands speak for you, so let them say the nicest possible things—always.

THE MANICURE

Line up your tools: polish remover, emery board, cuticle softener, a bowl of warm sudsy water, nail brush, small cuticle scissors, a fine-tipped orange stick, hand cream or lotion, a base coat and nail enamel. If you use a dry polish, you will need a nail buffer and a paste or dry powder for shine.

STEP 1. Dampen a piece of cotton with polish remover, or use a polish-remover pad. If some of the polish remains around the edges of your nails, remove it carefully with a cotton-tipped orange stick dipped in the remover.

STEP 2. With an emery board, file your nails to a rounded oval shape. If they have a tendency to split, use the fine-grained side of the emery board to level the layers. Don't file your nails too far down at the edges, and be sure to file gently in only one direction.

STEP 3. Apply a cream or oil cuticle remover at the base of each nail. Remember, a little of it goes a long way. Gently push back the cuticle with the fine tip of an orange stick. Make cuticle cream a habit; it will help prevent hangnails and ragged cuticles.

STEP 4. Take a few minutes to soak each hand in warm, sudsy water and scrub your nails with a brush. Dry with a soft towel and gently push back the cuticle. This should be done whenever you wash your hands, if time permits. This is also a great opportunity to treat your hands and your arms up to your elbows to a generous dash of hand cream or lotion.

STEP 5. Now trim off your hangnails, if any, with small cuticle scissors. Try not to cut into the cuticle itself, as this toughens it and encourages more hangnails.

STEP 6. Dip your nails into the water again to remove every last bit of cream. Again, push the cuticle back with a towel.

STEP 7. If you're going to buff or repair nails, this is the time to do it.

STEP 8. Apply the base coat to your nails. If you are able to do so, it's worthwhile to let polish dry thoroughly between coats.

STEP 9. Apply two coats of enamel, using as few strokes as possible. Use the polish sparingly; one dip in the bottle for each nail should be enough. Stroke with the brush from the base of your nail to the tip. The first stroke goes down from the center of the nail, then one down each side. You can use a top coat, if you wish; the result will be longer-lasting and a bit shinier. It is better to apply several thin coats than one heavy one; the polish will dry quicker and last longer and help to strengthen the nails.

STEP 10. For a clean finish, run a cotton-tipped orange stick dampened with polish remover along the outside of the cuticle to remove any smudges of polish. Make sure your nails dry for at least one half hour so that you won't have to reapply polish. A fast-drying spray or sealer will speed the action.

MENDING A NAIL

If you've chipped, cracked or split a nail and it looks as though it could be saved, don't cut it off. You can keep a special ready-made nail-repair kit on hand, or you can mend your nail with the tools you have at home —a trick I learned from a manicurist at a famous salon. You can use a fibrous paper such as one for cleaning eyeglasses. I prefer to use a piece of handkerchief linen. (Cotton won't do, as it's too heavy and not porous enough.) Tear or cut a small piece of linen or paper a little larger in size than the break, split or chip so that you can tuck a tiny bit of material under the nail. Brush the patch with airplane or household cement, place the wet side down on the nail and, taking your orange stick, lightly smooth the surface of the patch so that it is wrinkle-free. If you've used too much cement, use a minute bit of polish remover on the tip of the orange stick to remove all the bumps; if this doesn't work the first time, better start over again. To tuck the patch under your nail, put a small amount of cement on the edge and smooth it under the nail with the orange stick. Continue until there are no rough spots on the edge of the patch. Again, remember, polish remover on the tip of the orange stick helps in the smoothing. When the patch is completely dry, apply a base coat, followed by two coats of polish and a top sealer coat. The patch should be hardly discernible.

FALSE NAILS

Just one broken or shortened nail on lovely hands can be a disaster. That is why false nails might almost be considered a must in your makeup box. Although they are preshaped and come in sizes from slender to large, false nails usually need a bit more shaping. Use an emery board to custom-fit them to your own fingers—but be careful, for these nails can't grow back. When applying them, put glue on your own nail as well as on the inside of the false one. Wait until the glue is almost dry; then press the false nail onto your own. You will notice you can still move the nail back and forth. Let the false nails set in position before trying to use your hands in your normal tasks.

Though I have been using them and putting them on myself for more than ten years, Patti Nails or Liquid Nails are best applied by a specialist. Have it done professionally the first or second time, watch carefully, practice at home and you'll soon get the hang of it. Patti Nails and Liquid Nails are similar. To apply them, you first affix a horseshoe-shaped piece of aluminum to the end of the nail. The powder and liquid which come in the package you buy are mixed according to directions and brushed onto the "elongated" nails. When the nails are dry, they can be filed with an emery board and shaped to suit your own taste.

TIPS FOR HAND AND NAIL BEAUTY

1. Here are two remedies if the skin on your hands isn't as smooth and moisturized as it should be:

a. Rub baby oil into your hands before putting on rubber gloves to do the dishes or hand laundry. The heat from the water acts as a catalyst in working the soothing, smoothing agents of the oil into the pores.

b. Give your hands a rubdown with petroleum jelly before going to bed and wear gloves to keep the jelly from rubbing off. Special sleeping mitts for this purpose may be purchased in the notions department of most stores.

2. Wear rubber gloves when doing household chores.

3. Ink, nicotine and other stains can be removed from your fingers by rubbing with a cut lemon. For a stubborn stain, rub with a cotton swab dipped into laundry bleach. Be sure to rinse your hands right away by running them under cold water for a full minute. Then slather on cream to prevent them from becoming dry.

4. To make fake nails more pliable and to curve them so that they fit your own nails exactly, immerse them in hot water for a few minutes.

5. Use a moist pumice to rub away calluses at the sides of nails. An extra-fine pumice can be used to smooth away the very last rough edges on the tips and sides of the nails after filing.

6. Frosted nail polish is not the best lacquer for healthy nails, but that doesn't mean you should stop using it. Just be sure to protect your nails by using two applications of base coat instead of one.

7. When applying nail polish you'll find that the brush works more efficiently when excess polish does not drip down from above.

8. You can make your bottle of polish last longer by wiping off the neck of the bottle after use.

9. Give your nails a chance to breathe by removing old polish before going to sleep and applying new polish in the morning.

10. Darker shades of polish call more attention to the nails. If you prefer to wear a deeper color, your nails should be long, all the same length and perfectly shaped. With long nails, such as I have, I polish the undersides of the tips too. For photographs, it really does make a great difference.

11. Eat lots of protein foods such as meats, eggs, cheese and milk for healthy nails.

12. If you suffer from soft, splitting or cracking nails, get more protein in your diet by adding a gelatin capsule to juice; or better yet, buy gelatin drinks that come in fruit flavors.

13. Use something other than your fingertips for dialing the phone, and learn to unfasten your jewelry clasps with a tweezer.

14. Emery boards are best for filing the nails, since nail files can scratch the surface.

15. Unhealthy nails should be filed square, with the sides straight out for support until they can grow long enough to be shaped into pretty ovals.

16. Make it a regular habit to use hand cream each time you wash your hands. Carry a small tube or plastic bottle of your favorite product in your handbag or briefcase.

17. Always try to keep your fingers relaxed—no clenched fingers or fists, even while you're sleeping. This will keep your knuckles small and smooth. Big, knotty knuckles do not belong on pretty hands.

PUT A BEAUTIFUL FOOT FORWARD

There's hardly a thing that will make you feel more pampered than a pedicure.

Pretty feet count, for you want to be as perfect as you can from head to toe. During the sandal season you should be able to bare your toes with pride. A model keeps her feet as attractive as her hands. Here are the steps to an easy, perfect pedicure as well as some tips to keep your toes in top condition. They should look pretty and feel good at all times.

1. Start by applying cuticle remover to the edges of your toenails. Wait a few minutes; then soak your feet in a tub filled with warm soapy water to which you have added a drop or two of bath oil. Soak for another few minutes. This softens dead skin and cuticle and make the nails easier to cut.

2. If you have unusually rough heels, calluses and dead skin on the bottoms of your feet, take time to smooth them away with a moist pumice stone or an abrasive cream or lotion.

3. Clip your toenails straight across. (This helps to prevent ingrown toenails.)

4. File your nails smooth. If the nails on your big toes are thickened and ridged, use the coarse side of the emery board to refine them.

5. Push the cuticle back with a cotton-covered orange stick.

6. Give your feet a good rubdown with moisturizing lotion after every bath or shower. This keeps dry skin at a minimum.

7. Now, if you like polish, you are ready to apply it. Tuck small wads of facial tissue between your toes to keep the nails from smearing. Remove it only when your polish is positively dry.

TIPS

1. Make cooling foot-refresher sprays a part of daily foot grooming. If your feet are always on the go, carry a small can of spray in your handbag or briefcase. If you are out of foot spray, you can give your feet a rubdown with alcohol or cologne.

2. If your feet swell in the heat, it is a good idea to have a pair of sandals or shoes that are a half size larger in your wardrobe.

3. Always buy shoes that fit properly and are absolutely comfortable when you try them on in the store.

4. See a foot specialist at the first sign of discomfort.

5. Carry an extra pair of shoes with you if you spend a lot of time on your feet. A change of heel height will relax your feet.

6. Elevate your feet when you get home after a busy day; only a few minutes will rest them considerably.

7. For a really tingly and refreshed feeling, give your feet a facial mask. Cover your feet and ankles with the mask, prop them on a pillow and let

them rest there until they dry. Rinse with cold water and spray with cooling cologne, spray powder or a foot powder.

Following this skin care from inside out with diet and from top to toe with the preparations at hand, on a regular basis, will give you the good humor, efficiency and vitality you need to face every day with a sense of satisfaction.

CHAPTER 7

Model-Tested Hair Care

Beautiful hair is as essential to a model as well-balanced proportions and clear, fresh skin. In fact, one of America's super models admits, "I spend more time thinking about my hair than about any other aspect of my personal appearance. In my opinion there's nothing more beautiful than springy natural hair."

Of all beauty attributes, hair is one of the most noticeable—a perfect frame for a lovely face. One really wonderful advantage is that it *can* be arranged in ever so many ways. A hairdo can make you look taller, younger, more mature, fresher; bring out your prettiest features and minimize those which are less attractive. You can transform your hair from curly to straight and from straight to curly. But to make the most of your own gleaming locks, you must take proper care of your hair and scalp, so that you can recognize abnormalities and cope with any problems that arise.

HEALTHY HAIR

Healthy hair, like beautiful skin and strong nails, starts with diet. Since hair is protein, it makes sense to maintain its beauty by proper protein intake. Foods like chicken, lamb, pork and oysters give you a fine supply of the B vitamins you need for strong hair. Seafood containing iodine is especially valuable for good circulation, which nourishes the scalp.

Until recently, brushing was next to diet in importance. Nowadays, however, many experts postulate that the time-honored one hundred strokes can actually be detrimental. Prolonged brushing can split and break the ends of the healthiest hair. Scalp massage is suggested instead. If done properly it will be as salutary as good brushing, without the negative side effects. Here's how.

Sit in a comfortable position and prop your elbows on a table to keep them firm. Spread your fingers along your hairline and at the back of your neck. With your fingertips—not your fingernails—knead your scalp with tiny, circular movements. Work up from the nape of your neck to the front of your hairline. Then spread your fingers over the sides of your head above the ears and work up to the top of your head with the same circular motion. If your hair is oily, use less vigorous action than if your hair is dry or normal: barely move your scalp. This takes only a couple of minutes and leaves your scalp feeling refreshed and tingling.

This doesn't mean that you put brushing completely out of your beauty routine forever. First of all, hair needs a light brushout before and after washing. After a set, brushing eases the wave so that it looks more natural. Lots of women prefer a brush to a comb for smoothing their hair and keeping it in place. Nothing takes the place of swinging-clean hair, but if you're short of time, once in a while just cover the bristles of your brush with a layer of nylon stocking or cheesecloth and stroke gently through your scalp to pick out the dust and grime. Be careful to reposition the cloth on the brush every few strokes: you want to remove the dirt, not redistribute it. It's unwise to brush your hair when it's wet or damp—it's more fragile then than when it's dry.

Keep your brushes and combs spanking clean. Every few days (more often, if necessary) dip them into a solution of soapsuds, aromatic spirits of ammonia and lukewarm water. Swish them back and forth in the solution, brush them clean with an old soft toothbrush or nail brush and rinse them in cool water. In drying brushes, take care not to crush the bristles; stand them in a jar or glass until they're ready for reuse.

One word about hair health. If you have persistently bad dandruff or unusual amounts of falling hair, see your doctor. Some physiological factors may be causing the problem. He'll recommend a hair-care program just for you. Follow it. However, don't dash to his office if you see a few hairs on your comb or brush—that's normal. In fact, one expert says that up to a hundred falling hairs per day is normal for a person with a thick crop of hair.

CLEAN HAIR FOR BEAUTY

Hair has a "complexion" too: a fresh, shining complexion that just isn't evident unless it is scrupulously clean. That means regular shampooing. But what is "regular"? The word stands for something different for each person. Its meaning depends upon type of hair (dry, oily or normal), weather, life-style and geography.

Once a week is average, but that may take the life out of hair that's already dry. People with dry hair may wash it only once every two weeks or ten days, while those with oily hair have to shampoo more often—maybe twice a week or as often as every other day. Oily hair attracts dirt. Heads should be washed more frequently in the summer months than in cool weather, as they perspire more and heat tends to stimulate activity in the oil glands. Active-sports enthusiasts might have to shampoo frequently. In the city, where air is heavy with pollution, hair doesn't stay clean as long as it does in fresh country areas. When it comes right down to it, you're the only one who can judge just how often a head wash is called for. It doesn't take any special magic to know when the moment comes.

TIPS FOR HAIR CARE

Too many women just slick on shampoo and rinse it out. They are merely touching the surface. A few tricks can help you keep your hair clean for a longer period of time. Here's how models shampoo:

1. Massage the scalp.
2. Comb hair into place.
3. With a fine-toothed comb, gently scrape the scalp free of loose dandruff.
4. Wet the entire head with warm water.
5. Lather the entire head.
6. Rub shampoo in vigorously, using either fingertips or a rubber scalp brush.
7. Make a special point of working shampoo into the hairline. This area is apt to be the dirtiest and most neglected.

8. Rinse the hair in warm water.

9. Apply shampoo a second time. Work it in once again and rinse in cool water. For dry or normal hair, this should be sufficient, but for oily hair, shampoo a third time, rub, work in and rinse very thoroughly with warm water.

10. Rinse once more with cool water. To make sure all soap is gone, pull a strand of hair: if it squeaks, it's clean.

11. Conditioning rinse is a must for all types of hair. Protein rinses are best for normal hair. They add body and luster and prevent it from flying. A small amount is all that is required for best results. First, dissolve one-half capful in eight ounces of warm water. Now, starting two inches from the scalp, apply the rinse down to the ends of the hair. Take a large-toothed comb and stroke through the hair to distribute the rinse evenly. Next, rinse thoroughly with warm water for about one minute. Follow with a final rapid cold-water rinse for added sheen.

Special rinses are available for bleached, streaked or otherwise chemically treated hair. They too facilitate the combing of wet, tangled hair and give your hair body and sheen. They are applied and rinsed with the same procedure as for normal hair. Special conditioning rinses should be alternated frequently so that the hair doesn't become unresponsive.

12. After conditioning, gently rub your hair semidry with a thick terry towel and comb it through, being especially careful when working out snarls. Now you're ready to set your hair or arrange it in a hairstyle of your choice.

SPECIAL HAIR PAMPERING

DRY HAIR

Before shampooing, warm some olive or castor oil. Section your hair. Dip absorbent cotton into the warm oil and apply it all over your scalp, working from section to section; you'll be better able to saturate your whole scalp with this method. Wrap your head in a warm wet towel and wait at least twenty minutes. Then shampoo your head with warm water and a mild, oil-based soap: there are many fine products on the market made specifically for dry hair—or use a pure castile-soap shampoo. Be sure to wash out all excess oil or your hair will feel gooey. Follow with cream rinse for added manageability.

Dry hair has to be treated gently. No yanking, pulling, brush rollers or tough towel drying. Massaging your scalp often will be very helpful; it stimulates the oil glands. Don't expose dry hair to the sunlight for too long a time. A longer period under a medium- or low-temperature hair dryer is more beneficial than speed under a faster-drying, hot one. When you swim, shower or bathe, wear a cap. And make it a practice never to use water to keep stray hairs in place: this increases dryness. If you can, give yourself a treatment with a conditioning cream regularly once a week, and try to arrange for heat-cap treatments at your hairdresser's once in a while to prolong the beauty of your hair.

OILY HAIR

Wrap your head in steaming-hot towels for ten minutes before shampooing. Use an egg or detergent shampoo, and wash and rinse at least three times. (Be careful not to use a shampoo that's too strong or full of alcohol. Your oil glands will work twice as hard to compensate.) Wash your hair as often as necessary. In emergencies, use one of the dry shampoos or a liquid dry cleaner, or wipe strands of hair with cologne-saturated cotton. Stay away from fatty or spicy foods, which stir up your oil glands. Binding hats keep air from your scalp, so have that in mind when you select an Easter bonnet.

ANY-HAIR CARE

An egg shampoo is a real treat. The formula has been handed down to us by our great-grandmothers. You may end up with scrambled eggs on your head instead of beautiful, shining hair if you don't know just how to do it. Separate two or three eggs and whip the whites until peaks form. Add a tablespoon of water to the egg yolks and blend until the mixture is creamy. Then combine the beaten whites and yolks. Wet your hair with *warm* water. Gently pat away excess moisture with a towel. Apply part of the mixture to your damp hair. Let it set for a few minutes. Rinse your hair in *cool* water (not warm or hot—you don't want to cook the eggs). Keep applying the mixture until all of it has been consumed, and rinse until every bit of egg has disappeared. Pat your hair dry.

HIGHLIGHT RINSES

Highlights give hair a three-dimensional quality—real sparkling life. Here's how models get dazzling intensity.

BLONDS

A simple lemon rinse does wonders. Strain the juice of two lemons through cheesecloth; then mix with an equal amount of warm water. Rinse your hair with it after shampooing, and unless your hair is dry, leave it on. Sun damages colored hair, but if your hair is *naturally* blond, dry it in the sun.

REDHEADS

There's hardly anything more scintillating than amber highlights in clean, swingy hair. One natural redhead we know sparks up her own hair by brewing camomile tea as directed on the package, straining it and mixing it with a pint of water. She pours it through her hair and rinses with warm water. You can do the same.

BRUNETTES

A vinegar rinse brings out deep highlights in dark hair. Add four table-spoons of cider vinegar to three glasses of warm water, and massage the mixture gently through your hair. Rinse with cool water to remove the odor. A few drops of cologne in the last rinse water guarantee pretty-smelling tresses.

NOTE: Many models use natural colorless henna as a rinse. Not only is it a splendid conditioner, it also intensifies and accentuates the sparkle of *any* color hair.

HAIRSTYLES

The styling of your hair is pretty much a question of current fashion and your own taste. Though hair can be used to compensate for an imperfect feature (see some tricks that follow), try not to become a slave to restrictive tradition. It's more useful to experiment with different styles and learn to judge objectively which ones enhance your looks. It's a more exciting way to approach a hairdo that is really "you."

Whatever length or style you prefer, have your hair professionally cut or trimmed. The basis of all good-looking, long-lasting hairstyles is a super cut. Find the best coiffeur in your area and give him an idea of what you're looking for; he'll take over from there. You needn't have your hair done professionally each week—that could wreck most budgets —but with a good basic cut, it will be easier for you to handle your hair alone. It's more economical, too; you won't require cutting or trimming so often.

The frequency of salon visits depends mainly on the length of your hair and only partially on its style. Short hair, worn shaped to the head in back, may need to be trimmed every three or four weeks. A medium-length haircut can often hold its shape six weeks. Long hair may need only to be trimmed an inch or so every three months. Your stylist is the master of several cutting methods and will know which is suitable for you. *Blunt cutting* means using a scissors to cut straight across the ends. This is an excellent technique for fine, thin, soft hair or hair that has split ends. *Tapering* means using either scissors or razor to cut across the hair at an angle. *Layering* means cutting hair at a succession of different lengths. Sometimes, for short ruffled, curly or wavy styles, layering is combined with tapering. An experienced stylist will cut hair (usually while wet) according to the direction in which it grows.

CAMOUFLAGE TRICKS YOUR STYLIST CAN USE TO MAKE YOU PRETTIER

FOR

LOW FOREHEAD: Either sweep your hair clear off your forehead or if you like bangs, keep them short and high, rounded or separated.

HIGH FOREHEAD: Bangs are perfect—fluffy, separated bangs or side-swept bangs. Wispy curls around the hairline area are fine too.

Model-Tested Hair Care

NARROW FOREHEAD: Keep hair away from the sides of your forehead. Don't clutter your forehead with curls or waves.

BROAD FOREHEAD: Cover the sides of your forehead with soft curls, waves or sweeps of hair. Don't pull all your hair away from your face.

LONG NOSE: Stick to soft styles, gently waved or curled, with a little height at the crown. Fluffy bangs, not flat ones, will help too. Avoid center parts or fullness at the back of your head.

SHORT NOSE: Don't hide your face under long bangs or wear lots of hair around it. A short, fluffy style is probably best.

PLUMP CHEEKS: Keep your hair close to your head at the sides; that will give the effect of shadows your cheeks don't have.

THIN CHEEKS: Try for fullness at the sides of your face, but do not let curls or softness close in on your cheeks. You can also pull your side hair back, leaving only a few tendrils or soft curls.

SQUARE JAW: Soften the shape of your face with fluffy curls or waves at the sides of your head somewhat higher than your jawline.

HEAVY JAW: Keep your jawline free of curls or waves; rather concentrate on curls, waves or softness about temple level.

RECEDING CHIN: Don't sleek back your hair into a twist, bun or whatever. Bring your hair toward your face and wear it full at the back.

SHARP CHIN: Keep your hair free of your chin line. Add height and fullness at the top of your head to keep attention away from your chin.

SKINNY NECK: Fill out your neckline with long hair.

PLUMP NECK: Keep your hair clear of your neckline. Wear a short, simple style.

LONG NECK: Steer clear of short hairstyles unless your neck is in proportion with the rest of your size and it is smooth and young-looking.

SHORT NECK: Long hair suffocates your proportions, so stay away from very long hair. Medium or short styles are best for you.

Whatever style you choose, there are three "nevers." Never overtease, overspray or overexpose your hair to sunlight. These are the three most insidious deterrents to hair health. No style can be beautiful if your hair isn't in good condition. Instead of teasing, bend from your waist and gently brush your hair upside-down. This fluffs the hair without matting it as teasing does. If your hair needs a touch of something to keep it in place, moisten a cotton puff with spray and lightly touch over the top of your hair. This tames flying wisps without creating that "don't touch" rigidity of direct spraying.

COLOR MAGIC

There's hardly a model who doesn't use a little color magic once in a while. The right color, properly applied, can do wonders for hair, skin, eyes and even a case of the blues. However, wrong color can only be a disaster. Know what you're doing before you decide to try a color change.

If you want darker hair, try out a rinse. If you don't like it, you're not stuck until your natural hair grows out: it washes away. Another test: if you want to go lighter or darker, try on several wigs of different color to see which pleases you most.

To look natural, the new color has to complement your skin tone. Women over thirty look more attractive with hair just slightly lighter than their natural shade. Most skins tend to fade with added years, and darker tones may be too harsh. Only those who possess the very palest skin look pretty with red hair. Olive-complexioned women should steer clear of red and blond shades to avoid that lackluster look. Those with sallow complexions should stay away from blond tones; warm browns are best. Unless you have time for very *regular* touch-ups, stay fairly close to your own shade. Bright red, pitch black and brassy blond hair are obvious "dye jobs." The point is to look as naturally radiant as possible.

When you have chosen a new color, it's wise to have it done professionally the first time. If you can't afford regular visits to the salon, watch closely. Next time you can do it yourself, but *follow the instructions on the box to the letter.* You're a novice working with chemicals, while the manufacturer draws on long scientific experience to determine what these chemicals do and how long they take to develop on the hair.

TEMPORARY RINSES do a good job in eliminating minor discolorations, toning bleached or tinted hair and highlighting your natural hair color. They tone down brassy shades and add warmth to dull or mousy ones. Before coloring, give yourself a preliminary patch test to be sure you won't have an allergic reaction to any ingredient in the rinse. Make a second test to see how your hair reacts to the solution by using a strand from the center back of your head, where the hair is most natural. The period of time over which the color will hold depends upon the particular rinse you use. Some rinses last only until the next shampoo; others, called semipermanent rinses, gradually lighten over a period of four to six weeks.

PERMANENT TINTS are trickier and more difficult to deal with because they actually change your entire hair color—lighter or darker as you intend. Lighteners do just what the name implies. They only lighten the hair, *not* dye it. If your hair is light brown and you want to be a blond, lightener is not for you, but if you want a sun-streaked look, then a lightener is your best bet. Lighteners act to remove color from the hair in varying degrees. This depends on the strength of the product. If your hair is not normally done by a professional colorist, it would at least be a good idea to consult one before you choose a lightener.

PREBLEACHES remove color from your hair prior to application of a toner that recolors it to any of the pale shades. This two-step method is prescribed for brunettes who want to be blonds. Color is first applied to the roots and then smoothed out toward the ends.

TIPPING requires the selection and lightening of small strands of hair around the hairline. Let a color expert do this for you.

FROSTING may be another attractive response to your demand for change. It's tipping of the hair on the entire head. Here's something to watch for: if the streaks in tipping or frosting can be counted, it's a sure giveaway that you've done it yourself. Professionals achieve a smooth glazed effect. These tinging and lightening processes last until the hair grows out.

Once your hair is colored, don't neglect the upkeep. Touch up whenever necessary—every month or six weeks. Give attention to conditioning treatments, especially if your hair is dry. And as I've said, be particularly careful to cover your head when you're in the sun. If you swim in salt water or a chlorinated pool, wear a cap and wash your hair as soon as possible or you may end up with a color different from the one you bargained for—green or orange.

CURLING OR STRAIGHTENING

Permanents have come a long way from the old crimpers that left hair hopelessly kinked and fuzzed. Straightening is a lot more practicable, too. But try to avoid both processes, unless you simply can't manage your hair. Again, their effectiveness depends on chemicals, and they can't help weakening even healthy hair. If hair isn't strong and good to start with, the chemicals may just be too much. If you're convinced that your hair requires straightening or a permanent to look its most attractive, proceed with utmost caution. Use conditioner on your hair a few times beforehand, and get into the habit of using it on a regular basis afterward. Read the instructions on the box before proceeding, and follow them *to the letter.* You're asking for real trouble if you improvise. A word of caution: straightening or permanent waving should be done at least one week before you color your hair or touch it up. *The two operations should never be done at the same time.*

A few last things to remember.

1. If your hair shows signs of damage, stop the coloring process and start conditioning. Keep it up until your hair regains its health.

2. Comb tangles starting from the outer ends and working in a little at a time toward the roots.

3. Plastic rollers are best for colored hair.

4. Before you change your hair color, consider the cost of the special grooming and upkeep in both time and money. Be honest with yourself. Don't color your hair if you tend to be lazy. You will probably regret it if you do.

The name of the game is beauty. A model can't afford to be seen with discolored roots and split, damaged ends. You can't afford it either. Establish a hair-coloring routine that gives you the drama you're looking for and stick to it!

CREATING THE RIGHT "FALSE IMPRESSION"

I'm actually mad about wigs and hairpieces. Countless times they have "saved" me socially and professionally. Offhand I would say that I have at least ten wigs, in addition to an assortment of falls, wiglets, braids—every hairpiece imaginable is in my hair wardrobe.

I originally became addicted to them when, as a model, I was required to modify my "look" at a moment's notice. Photographers and clients and, I suppose, husbands and boyfriends too become tired of the same old appearance all the time, so I am at an advantage when I can make a switch.

The basic portion of my personal hairdressing assortment was purchased before the advent of the marvelous new synthetic hairpieces and wigs available today at such modest prices. Most of my pieces are made from European hair. They were terribly expensive when I bought them. Believe me, were I to start once more, I would have in my wig closet only Dynel or Kanekalon modacrylic synthetic wigs of the stretch type. These wigs and hairpieces range in price from about $30 to about $50, come in an endless number of styles and colors and require almost no care.

When considering an investment in a wig, by all means do so intelligently. Don't buy anything just because it's cheap. I have found there are very few bargains in life. The few times I have tried to save a few pennies, I have had to sacrifice quality somewhere along the line.

Some guidelines on what to look for when shopping for synthetic wigs:

1. Try to examine the wig in the daylight. If it picks up unnatural colors such as pinks, purples or greens, put it back on the counter.

2. Check the wig carefully for natural luster. Avoid anything that is too dull or too bright.

3. The fiber should feel soft and similar to human hair. It's not for you if it is slick like the hair they put on dolls.

4. Even the best synthetic can be damaged in the dyeing and curl-baking process. This results in bristly hair. A good way to check this is to use a brush to see how the hair behaves. The best wigs move well and handle easily in every direction.

5. No matter how adventuresome you feel, always pick a wig that matches your skin coloring. Blonds may "have more fun," but not if they're unattractive. Create a new image if you want to, but please stay within the bounds of reality and good taste.

Most synthetic wigs have their curl baked in and need no resetting. Natural-hair types, however, *do* require attention. Use a setting lotion made specially for wigs and hairpieces. When wigs are made of real hair, a squirt of water is all that's necessary before you use each plastic roller. I set my own hairpieces by securing them to a wig stand; inexpensive ones of Styrofoam are to be found in most stores. Heated rollers can be used on a hairpiece, but I've found that if you utilize them too often, the hair becomes dry. Of course, there are no natural oils to remedy this. Should this happen to your hairpiece, you might give it a light touch of a cream dressing or spray conditioner—but *go easy, please.* You can spoil it for all time with too heavy a hand.

To remove surface dirt, brush the piece gently with a wig brush or one with soft bristles. The wig can be styled with this brush, too. If your hairpiece should become snarled, untangle it with a wide-toothed comb or a very large hairpin, working carefully from the ends or tips of the hair toward the base.

Don't wash a hairpiece of real hair. You can dry-clean it yourself with a special solution, but if you value its beauty, it's worth having it cleaned professionally. You can wash your synthetic pieces with shampoo and cold water very easily and with good results. Hold the piece by the base and lightly swish it through the suds. Rinse. Pat dry with towels, and hang it by the front to dry. You can put it in a mesh laundry bag to prevent snarls while it's being washed. If the wig base should get wet, put it on a block and don't comb the hair until the base is dry. The block will prevent it from shrinking.

A synthetic hairpiece cannot be recolored. Real hairpieces shouldn't be dyed either, but a rinse can be put on by a professional hairdresser or colorist. Don't try to do this yourself.

Keep hairpieces pinned to a wig stand. They should be kept away from heat and bright lights, because the hair will oxidize and change color. Keep the stand in a tall covered box, or tie a silk scraf around it loosely. It can be stored in a roomy plastic bag if you wish.

Other reminders:

1. Avoid permanents or straightening on hairpieces.
2. Don't use regular hair spray on them.

3. Make certain your hairpieces match your basic hair color.

In putting on a fall, switch or wiglet, make two or three pin curls of your own hair and crisscross them with bobby pins in the place to which you want to attach the hairpiece. Now slide the little comb attached to the piece under the pin curls and you're all set.

One of the most important factors in getting a soignée effect when you're putting on a wig—stretch or any other kind—is what you do with your own hair. I still think it is best to wind up your own hair neatly in pin curls and make one or two pin curls crisscrossed with bobby pins just a little past your front hairline to keep the wig from slipping. You can cover your head with a nylon stocking, but I find that isn't very comfortable. If you have long hair, pull your hair back and divide it into three strands. Twist each strand and pull it as flat as possible to your scalp. This eliminates any large bumps. Keep some hair out to make a small pin curl on each side of the temple and on top of your head so that the wig can be secured by the small combs usually attached to the front; or you can stick a hairpin carefully through the net to hold the wig in place. Now you are ready for the styling.

If the wig has bangs or soft curls that cover your forehead, you don't have to worry about your hairline. If you want to cover the hairline of the wig, do everything mentioned above, but leave a quarter inch of your own hair out around the hairline. This should be enough to brush over the wig line. If it's not, then try again, leaving more of your own hair showing. Don't overdo, however, for that can spoil the naturalness.

I have found that whether it's a short or long hairpiece you want to wear, a slight combing of your own hair over the front and sides makes the entire styling more attractive.

For ten years now I have been doing my own wigs and pieces, and I've become quite adept. Still, once every three cleanings, I take them all into my hairdresser. He uses little trade secrets or a new style I hadn't even thought of that keeps my wigs and hairpieces fresh and fashionable. I advise you to follow my lead.

If you haven't thought of owning and wearing a wig, fall or other hairpiece until now, I hope I've convinced you that they are fun, great timesavers and really worth trying.

A good crop of fresh, clean hair, any length, and a supply of becoming wigs and hairpieces allow you to be your most attractive, well-groomed self for all occasions. Whether the events are planned well in advance or take place on a moment's notice, *you* are always ready.

CHAPTER 8

Model-Tested Makeup

Cosmetics are the mere tools used in the art of makeup. They are intended to enhance and beautify the natural you as well as accentuate features that may otherwise remain unnoticed. But in truth it is the hands which manipulate these tools that are the major factor in determining the end result.

Models must be artists to understand the cosmetic needs of their own faces and to meet the challenge presented by makeup problems they encounter on their assignments. For the model, on- and off-camera makeup are two completely different schemes. What appears natural to the eye of the camera looks heavy, sometimes even clownlike, in everyday life. Both kinds of makeup follow the same basic principles. Exaggerations, however, are strongly avoided for street wear, and a model buffs and polishes her finished makeup so that she looks as clean, fresh and naturally healthy as possible. She knows that the real trick is to look beautiful, not beautifully made up. It takes time and practice, but once the techniques are mastered, no more than eight to twelve minutes are needed to "do your face." This chapter is about what you do in that short period of time to make yourself alluring.

Amy Green, former beauty editor for both *Glamour* and *McCall's* magazines, once referred to me as "the best makeup artist I have ever known." With this professional accolade to commend my skill, let me pass along to you some cosmetic magic as I know it and as I practice it every day of my life.

Before seeking the makeup that is right for you, establish two things: First, what kind of skin do you have—dry, normal or oily? Second, what is your natural coloring?

I strongly advise seeking professional advice as to the latter. It is not the tone of the foundation and other cosmetics you buy that creates the final effect of beauty when your makeup is completed, but rather the combination of your natural coloring with the colors you have added. For example, if one uses an olive foundation over an olive complexion, a totally undesirable "yellowing" effect will result. The same holds true if one possesses pinkish tones in the skin and uses a color containing pink. The countenance gives the impression of one long, continuous, embarrassing blush. Always strive for balance of color between natural skin tones and added color in cosmetics.

It is vital that your entire "wardrobe" of cosmetics be coordinated with respect to tint and consistency of oils. An incorrect shade of powder over an ideally suited foundation can be disastrous, and the reverse is also true. The same applies to blushers, rouges and lip colorings. What you need is a personalized, color-coordinated beauty kit. If you need professional help to get it together, many beauty experts are available in your local department stores waiting to give you counsel of the best sort.

MODEL'S BEAUTY KIT

Your beauty kit doesn't have to cost a fortune, nor is a duffel bag full of cosmetics necessary or desirable. High-quality tweezers, lash curlers and manicuring instruments are worthwhile investments, for they last a long time. Cleansing lotions, astringents, moisturizers and foundations can be purchased in economy sizes. A wise makeup shopper, once she knows her proper color scheme, buys cosmetics in a cut-rate drugstore, and she hunts for excellent products that can be found in variety stores at a fraction of what more highly advertised products cost elsewhere.

Now for your beauty basics:

Cleansing lotion or cream
Moisturizer
Foundation (three shades: skin-toned, lighter and darker)
Transparent powder, loose or pressed
Powder puffs or cotton balls
Blusher, creamy and brush-on
Lipstick and/or lip gloss
Eyelash curler

Tweezers
Mascara, cake or roll-on
Eye shadow, one color or a collection, if you like variety
Eye liner and brush
Cotton-tipped swabs
Eyebrow makeup: pencil or, if needed, lightening powder
Eyebrow and lash brush
Magnifying/regular mirror
Eyelashes, if you like them
Manicure set

Keep these in a handy case in the bathroom or on your dressing table —wherever you feel most relaxed and comfortable when making up.

FOUNDATION

After moisturizer, which needs no comment, foundation is the base of all makeup. It hides small flaws and even poor skin coloring. In addition, it acts as protection from the elements—wind, sun and water. It goes without saying that moisturizer and foundation should always be applied to clean, clear skin.

Here are the cosmetic-artistry hints I promised.

When I have cleansed and moisturized my skin thoroughly, I put on a very thin layer of liquid foundation using a sponge so that it's practically invisible. I blend it into my hairline, ears, and neck so that all my exposed skin has a sameness of tone, but I advise nonmodels to follow a slightly different method.

For your base shade, choose a color that's as close as possible to your skin tone. Shake it well and dot it on your forehead, nose, chin and each cheek. With your second finger, spread the foundation gently in an upward, outward motion until it is completely blended. (The up-out movement keeps delicate face muscles from being unalterably pulled down.)

Younger women who want a more natural look might well use one of the new tinted moisturizers instead of foundation, while older women with flawless skins really need no foundation and can eliminate this step, if they choose.

Once my foundation is in place, I use an erasing stick to fill in the little laugh lines I wish to minimize. I blend the erasing-stick color into the foundation carefully so that there are no color demarkations. Then I set the basic cosmetics—moisturizer and foundation as well as erasing stick—with transparent powder.

If there are other transitory situations with which I am discontent and which I want to correct cosmetically, I use a few little tricks before my powdering. For example, if I notice dark circles under my eyes, I correct them by going against precedent. Most experts recommend using a lighter shade under the eyes before applying regular foundation; I totally disagree, since highlighting generally brings attention, which is what, in this case, I want to avoid. I apply a slightly *darker* shade of foundation under my eyes and apply my regular foundation color over it. The result is much more natural and doesn't create a "fish-eye" look. If you smile a lot and are getting little wrinkles under your eyes, as I am, makeup and powder only tend to accentuate the problem. Not all is lost, however. Here is what I do.

Before applying foundation and powder, I pat a small amount of good, rich eye cream over the area. A lubricating effect is created, and the skin is kept pliant and moist all during the day and evening. If the area under my eyes begins to shine, I use a makeup blotter, but I never, never re-powder. The same goes for other danger points.

During the entire time I am at work or at recreation, I keep a sharp lookout around the areas of my nose and chin. The minute I see the shine that indicates an excess of oil, out comes one of those lovely little face blotters again. They absorb the moisture and oils and remove the shine without removing the makeup I have put on so carefully in the morning. I wouldn't be without them. Again, no repowdering of the nose or other areas of the face during the day or evening, or you'll look masklike and very unattractive.

But let's return to our basic makeup.

The right moment at which to use setting powder depends on the kind of blushers, shadings and rouges you prefer. Creams or liquids should usually be applied *before* powdering. Cakes and powders should always be applied *afterward*. For the most part I prefer cake-powder types, because they can be used with various brushes that give better control and subtlety in feathering. (However, if I need special effects, I sometimes break these rules.)

Over my foundation and my "tricks" I apply a sheer, no-color trans-lucent powder. I press lightly, using the powder sparingly. (I never rub the powder on my skin.) Then I eliminate the excess using a special powder brush. This results in a dull, slightly powdery illusion at first, but it quickly disappears when the natural oils of my skin begin to come through and give off an imperceptible glow.

CONTOURING

At this point, I begin to highlight and lowlight the various planes of my face with rouges, blushers and shadows.

Even the most beautiful model rarely has perfect features, and to some extent contouring helps nature out. The contouring techniques themselves are based on the principle that light draws attention while dark detracts from it. To bring out a beautiful feature, use a lighter base. To diminish an unattractive one, use darker foundation. This has to be done very subtly. If it's obvious, it will only accentuate an imperfection that you wish to hide. Liquid contouring colors should be blended carefully into the makeup prior to powdering. Since I use cake-powder contouring colors, I apply them *after* the powder, using a makeup brush specially designed for blending and feathering powdered products. I put the rouge or blusher on the high point of my cheekbones, utilizing the smallest possible amount. I work the contouring color into my hairline following the line of my cheekbone. Next, I blend it down to obtain a smooth, gradual effect in all directions. When I want a slight glowing effect, I break the rules and apply cream or liquid blusher over a foundation that has already been powdered and set.

I advise you to experiment with different ways of contouring so that each of your loveliest features will be brought out to the fullest degree. By trial and error you can decide on liquid or cake colorings that do the best job for you.

For young women or those with trouble-free complexions, I suggest the use of the new tinted gels that blend so beautifully over moisturizer. They have a marvelous luminous warmth and are so very easy to handle.

SHADING

My shading comes after contouring. I use a brownish shade, in cake form. (You should select one with a slight tinge of pink, orange or red, depending upon your hair coloring.) The brown shadow is ever so fine-spun, and I brush it on with very light strokes under the cheekbone in a semireverse triangle. The widest part is next to the hairline and goes no lower than the bottom of the earlobe and no farther toward the nose than slightly past the outside edge of the eye. If you try shading, make sure you feather the color into that of your foundation so that it's impossible to see where one color leaves off and the other begins. If you think your jawline is too prominent, subdue it by shading under your chin and jawline. You can use the same trick on your nose. If you feel it's too wide, simply shade the sides, making sure that the color is practically indefinable and well feathered. Some models prefer to shade the temples just above the spot where the cheekbone and hairline meet. This technique, of course, depends on the structure of the face. You'll have to study the proper shading for your own special physiognomy. There should be emphasis on a natural look for daytime wear, but for evening a bolder, more dramatic, approach is certainly acceptable.

Here are a few eye-fooling tricks you might try.

BROAD NOSE: Blend a line of lighter makeup down the center of the nose; blend darker base along each side.

LONG FACE: Smooth lighter foundation
over your cheeks and forehead,
darker foundation over your chin and neck.

WIDE JAW: Apply darker makeup over
the wide part and blend.

LONG NOSE: Smooth a darker base under the tip of the nose.

ROUND OR SQUARE FACE: Apply darker foundation to the outer edges of your cheeks from ear to chin.

LOW FOREHEAD: Apply lighter makeup along your hairline.

HIGH FOREHEAD: Apply darker makeup along your hairline.

NARROW FACE: Apply a lighter shade to the outer edges of your cheeks from ear to chin.

RECEDING CHIN: Blend in a lighter
shade of foundation on your chin.

PROTRUDING CHIN: Blend in a darker
shade of foundation on your chin.

No matter what contouring and shading you do, finish off with a light dusting of powder applied with a clean puff or cotton ball. Use a soft brush, as always, to remove the excess. Blush your cheeks lightly with powder blusher and you're ready for the eyes.

EYES

Without lifting a finger or moving a muscle, a clever woman says more with her eyes than with her lips. Regardless of their size or shape, the eyes set the entire tone of who and what a woman is. They mirror her feeling and personality more quietly or blantantly than her gestures or her words, so knowledge of the proper application of eye makeup and practice in utilizing today's eye cosmetics in accordance with current fashion trends can enhance the genuine expression of the eyes tenfold. First and foremost, however, take note that skills which may be suitable for a very dazzling public personality, such as a model or an actress, may not be suitable for your own particular life-style. An insatiable curiosity about fashion will stand you in good stead while you're searching for the modes that work well for you. By all means make changes, but when fashion legislates against you in one season or another, continue to employ those colorations which augment your beauty. Leave exoticism to others for whom the styles might be more becoming.

There are literally dozens of products and specialized tools for the creation of fascinating eyes. Practically every eye size and shape has been analyzed by beauty experts seeking solutions to the particular problems of particular faces. Try them all, in small amounts. Pick out the ones that match your own eye forms and continue your search for makeup competence.

An entire book could be written on the subject, but for now, I'll just describe normal application of eye makeup as I practice it and add some special little hints that should be as useful to you as they have been to me.

Generally, eye makeup is put on in the following stages:

First, dark eye shadow is applied under the bone of the upper eye.

Second, light shadow is brushed onto the eyelid (if desired).

Third, eye liner is put on (optional also).

Fourth, false lashes (again optional).

Fifth, mascara is applied.

Finally, the eyebrow is made up to complete the eye picture.

Now let's go step by step through each stage.

Position your makeup mirror so that it is well lighted and you are looking straight into it. This makes it easy to do a professional job without frustrating repeats. Remember, every step requires delicacy of application.

EYE SHADOW

The color you choose and the way in which you treat eye shadow are pretty much a matter of taste and fashion. Ordinarily, discreet colors look best for daytime; they're the browns, grays, and toned-down jewel colors. For evening, more brilliant and resplendent colors are in order. Eye shadowing depends on the shape of the eye also. Women with puffy eyelids look prettier with darker colors—nothing light or glittery to bring attention to the fleshiness. Deep-set eyes come forward when pale shadow is placed just above the lashes and dark shadow is blended above the crease under the brow. For a heavy lid, reverse the procedure. Use a dark shade on the lower lid and light shadow just below the brow. With any of these artifices, blend very carefully. Eyes that look "drawn on" don't seem attractive, no matter what attempts have been made to make them more exquisite. In this regard, my feeling is that shadow which complements the natural eye color is more quietly alluring than that which contrasts. Perhaps that is because I am opposed to anything vulgar.

As a brunette, I do this: My initial step is to use dark brown eye-shadow stick, applying the color with a brush to the area above and behind the place where my lid fold begins. I take care that it does not extend beyond the upper area between lid fold and lower brow line. For evening wear I may use a light iridescent shade in this area, blending and feathering it into the brown, highlighting the arch for an effect that is usually captivating and elegantly sexy.

Next, I use a medium brown cream shadow and brush it onto my upper lid, taking special care to blend it with my fingertip in a fan shape outward and upward to the point where my brow ends. I blend it with my regular makeup because once again, I don't want to be able to see where one color ends and another begins.

EYE LINER

Eye liner is pretty much a matter of changing with the times. Some years it's "in," some years it's not. Some girls look better without liner at all, but those with small, light eyes profit greatly from a delicate line that defines. Liner should always be as close to the lash as possible and barely more than a sliver in width. Tiny dots of liner smudged together at the base of the lash gives the same illusion, but even more artfully. In any case, black liner can be considered too harsh for almost everybody.

When you're utilizing liner under your eyes—again, brown, blue or gray—smudge it for the same soft effect before it sets. Brush-drawn lashes below the eye are all right for evening if they are very tiny, but I never recommend them for daytime under any circumstances. If you wish to make your eyes seem larger, draw a tiny white line at the extreme inner and outer corners of each eye. That will open up the eye rather than limit it.

Before I begin lining my own eyes, I decide just how far I wish to extend the lines beyond the outer corners. I place a dot at each point with my pencil. I use an inexpensive Chinese writing brush and cake liner as my tools, since I have discovered that commercial eye-liner pencils are too hard for my particular lids. The same may be true for you, so be on the lookout for any irritation in this delicate area.

I gently stretch the lid from the outer corner of the socket, and starting at the inside corner of the eye, I make a fine line. At the center of the lid I gradually widen the color until I have reached the guide spot where the line is heaviest of all. I turn the tip of the line slightly upward. The first few times you try this yourself, you may get a jagged line, but keep on practicing and you'll soon be an expert. Personally I'm not in favor of a lower liner. I prefer a faint smudge of medium brown shadow applied under my lower lashes with a brush.

Now that my eyes are shadowed and lined, the next step is the application of my false eyelashes. Occasionally, I go without them, simply using the extender technique with mascara on my natural lashes. I shall explain that technique in proper sequence.

FALSE EYELASHES

In front of the camera models feel practically undressed without false eyelashes, but off-camera that same kind of false lash looks heavy and unreal; it blacks out the eye area rather than making it seem larger. So they utilize the sparsest lashes they can find, or better yet, lashes put on in small groups, practically one at a time. They buy long strips of lashes and cut them according to need, or they cut up pairs of eyelashes to suit themselves, snipping the base of the lash about every one-sixteenth to one-eighth of an inch. If you try this for yourself, you'll have tiny lash strips with about five to fifteen lashes in each section.

When you buy lashes, either in strip or in ready-to-use form, match the color to your own and the heaviness to your personal taste, remembering what the model does about being subtle. Examine the string or base to which the lashes are attached. If it is too heavy it will require much too much glue, be clumsy to handle and call for too heavy an eye liner. A sure sign of good quality is a hairline base, the thinner the better. Lashes are even available with a skin-colored base for the no-liner look.

When trimming lashes, do keep in mind that natural lashes are never perfectly even at the edges, and they are most certainly not so thick as to resemble a fringe of hair. Avoid cutting lashes straight across. Natural lashes are shorter close to the nose and gradually become longer as they approach the outer corner of the eye. Try to approximate this natural contour of the lash. Do not use a pair of tiny cuticle scissors. Rather, use a single-edge razor blade and gently scrape the tips until you obtain a fine tapered end. This takes a little extra time, but the natural-looking result is worth the extra skill and care.

For the look of nature, there should always be some balance between the lashes of the upper and lower lids. If you need lashes on top, then chances are the same problem exists on the lower lid. If you are unable to achieve balance by using mascara and builder on the lower lashes, then perhaps it might be a good idea to consider a few individual lower lashes. These are available in strip form also.

I use lashes I have pretrimmed according to the process I have just described. First I determine which strip of lashes goes on which eye by holding them up without glue. Then, I put a very small amount of eyelash glue or surgical adhesive on the tip of a bobby pin and spread a thin coating on the base of the lashes. I hold the strip with a pair of tweezers and put it in position as close to my own lashes as possible.

Starting on the inside of the lid, using the tip of the bobby pin, I gently but firmly begin to press the lashes into place. When the glue has dried, I do a little touch-up with my liner, making sure the appearance is as though it had all been there to begin with. Finally, before applying my mascara, I integrate my own lashes with those which are false.

Tiny lash clumps are applied in the same way. Starting at the center of the eyes, add as many little lash strips as you like, depending on the effect you want. I myself do not use bottom lashes except on very rare social occasions, but I certainly think others should wear them for balance.

Though I have never had them applied to my own eyes, there are professional beauticians who can and do apply individual false lashes, one at a time. They are guaranteed to last and stay on for two or three months, provided you follow the beautician's instructions for their care and preservation. You will not be able to wash and cleanse your face as you might normally do, and you must also learn to sleep in a certain position so as not to disturb them. They really look marvelous, exactly like your very own, and can be real timesavers if your life requires that you spend a minimum amount of time at your dressing table.

No matter whether you use full eyelash strips, clumps of lashes or individual lashes, by all means exercise caution when removing them. Please don't take them off with tweezers or fingernails. Grip them between the pads of your forefinger and thumb and peel them off gently from the outer edge toward the inner part of the eye. Another no-no: never sleep with false eyelashes on—unless they're ones that have been professionally applied to last several months. Ordinary lashes will certainly become misshapen. When you remove your false lashes be extremely careful not to lose a precious natural lash or two of your own.

When you purchase lashes, you may as well buy some professional eyelash cleaner too. It is easy to use and saves wear and tear on the lashes. Simply immerse them in the liquid for a few moments. Remove them with tweezers from the fluid and lay them out on a fresh tissue. Gently brush away the old glue and mascara so that they are fresh for reuse. I am a real tightwad about lashes and use mine until they literally fall apart.

Last but not least, a little trick for putting the curl back into your used false lashes, or making your new lashes more manageable. Dip them into warm water for a second or two and lay them flat on a tissue. Fold the tissue over the lashes, roll it around a pencil and secure it with a rubber band. Let the lashes remain in this position overnight. You'll be amazed at the fine result. In the case of individual lashes, you'll have to rely on the old tried-and-true eyelash curler.

NATURAL EYELASHES

Even if you weren't born with long, sweeping, silken eyelashes, you can still get the effect without resorting to false lashes. To make eyes look bigger and lashes seem longer, start with curling. It causes absolutely no harm to the lashes when done gently and correctly. Grip the lashes in the curler and hold. Count to between fifteen and thirty, depending upon how easily your lashes curl and how definite you want the upswing to be. For more gradual curl, grip the lashes in the curler at their base, count to about ten; move the curler to the middle of the lash, count to ten; then curl the tips for another count of ten. Don't squeeze the curler too firmly; you'll get crimped rather than softly upturned eyelashes, and if you are rough you can damage the hairs. To keep lashes in healthy condition, it's a good idea to tip them with petroleum jelly at night, but be sure to remove any residue before applying mascara in the morning. If you don't do a good job, the mascara will smudge below your eyes and create a raccoonlike appearance.

MASCARA

Now it's time for my next approach in the makeup-wizardry campaign. No matter what kind of mascara you use—cake or brush-on tube— applying it is a true test of a steady hand. Too many of us just flick our lashes through a mascara brush and call the job done. But that's hardly a good beginning. When properly utilized, mascara can be one of the most effective cosmetics in the beauty kit. Here's what models do to get that "femme fatale" look.

With a mascara-laden brush, tip the ends of your lashes. Black is best for just about everyone but the blondest blonds (those whose eyebrows and lashes are as blond as their hair). When you tip lashes, get every single lash across your eye—top and bottom, from the extreme inner corner to the outer corner. You'll be surprised to see how many lashes you really have if you get all the way out to the tiny hairs at the edges. After each lash is tipped, cover the rest of the lash from base to tip, top and bottom lashes. Start at the base and *slowly* brush toward the tip. "Slowly" is the key word. When it's done quickly, the mascara is more likely to clump. Dust your lashes lightly with powder. After the first coating dries, repeat with second and third coats of mascara, brushing them on very slowly, as you did the first, and powdering after each coating. If the lashes stick together, take a tiny brush and flick through the lashes gently until they separate. Some models spend as much time applying mascara as they do on all the rest of their makeup put together, but when you follow their lead and see what big eyes you seem to have, you'll agree that's the only way to create the stunning illusion you're looking for.

EYEBROWS

Now for the final episode in dramatizing the eye: the drawing of the eyebrow. When I first started to model, one of my biggest problems was what to do with my brows. Everyone had a different opinion, and I guess I was so insecure I listened to anyone I thought might know more about it than I did. First, I plucked them unmercifully and penciled them to a high arch. Next, I shortened them. Then I lengthened them. I made them fatter, then thinner. Nothing seemed right. Finally I took a vacation and was too lazy to do anything about them. What a happy surprise! My natural brow line was what I had been searching for after all. I had forgotten what it looked like. From then on it was a simple matter of tweezing out a few of the lower hairs to keep my brows from looking too scraggly, and that was that. I haven't changed much since, though in deference to the present softer look, I have bleached my brows a bit and use a light brown rather than the darker pencil I originally favored. It changes my "look" slightly, but basically, it's still the same old me.

It must be quite obvious by now that as the result of all my own unsuccessful experimentation, I am a strong champion of the natural brow line. You notice I didn't say natural brow, but rather brow line. Some brows are thick and bushy and require intelligent spare tweezing for a shaped, controlled natural outline. Here are some simple rules that will help you find the natural shape of your own brow. The ridge of your upper eye socket should indicate the natural brow line.

Draw an imaginary line from the widest part of your nose straight up to your hairline. The brow should ordinarily begin where the line crosses the hairs of the eyebrows. Tweeze away the extras.

Now, if you draw another imaginary, slightly diagonal, line from the outer corners of your eye across your temple to the upper edge of your ear, it will tell you where the brow should end. Make a pencil dot as your guide spot.

Now imagine a straight, level line from the outer tip of the right brow to the outer tip of the left brow. Both inner tips should touch the line also, and the line should be perfectly even.

If you have wide-set eyes, as I do, the high point of the arch should come somewhere directly above the outer edge of the iris, or colored part of your eye.

Thus you have a fairly good standard for defining your natural brow line. Try tweezing according to these suggestions. Be daring, if you don't like the effect. Change to another line you think more attractive, until you find the perfect one for your own expression.

Incidentally there are a few tweezing techniques that make the practice "painless" if you use a high-quality tweezer and a good magnifying mirror to increase your accuracy.

It is best to tweeze immediately after a facial sauna or a bath, when the pores are open. Hairs will come out easily.

Tweeze with the natural grain of the hair, not against it—otherwise you may encourage ingrown hairs. Don't tweeze the hairs above the arch, only those below.

After tweezing, it's wise to apply an antiseptic, or an astringent, such as witch hazel, to avoid the chance of infection.

When you've refined your brow into a clear-cut line, it's time to think about eyebrow makeup. Most people think in terms of darkening, but models learn early that brows need lightening in most cases. Heavy brows tend to give the impression of a scowl. Lightening can be done temporarily with a dusting of face powder or with one of the brow-lightening makeups on the market. When brows are very dark, consider having them bleached professionally. This is particularly good taste for women whose natural coloring is very, very dark, but who have changed hair color by bleaching or dying to a much lighter hue.

To sharpen your eyebrow pencils, file them so that they resemble the end of a screwdriver. I use two different colors, a medium brown, which I powder, and a slightly darker brown artist's pencil for drawing individual hairs. I use short, light strokes and fill in where needed following the natural direction of the hairs.

Light-haired lassies should never use black to darken brows. It's too harsh even for most brunettes. Use a brown, gray or beige pencil according to your hair coloring—or gold, if you want a glittery effect for evening. Follow the shape of the brow as closely as possible, and make light feathery strokes rather than solid lines at all times.

As a final touch, I use a dry eyelash brush to train my natural brows upward and outward.

That does it for the average eye. If you follow these ideas and suggestions, you should have the loveliest peepers in town. When that happens, be very careful how you use them. Beautiful eyes can be a very deadly pair of weapons in the pursuit of a Prince Charming. Aim well.

LIPS

The mouth is perhaps the most alluring, provocative feature of the face. As such it warrants special attention. Since there are an infinite number of shapes and sizes, a model must know how to enlarge thin lips and how to diminish thick lips to make them appear more delicate without the makeup technique's becoming obvious.

If your mouth is too large, too full, too thin, these problems can be corrected by knowledgeable application of lip liners, glosses and colors. (The diagrams will guide you in dealing with your own lovely mouth.)

Lip gloss or lip sheen livens up and moistens the appearance of even the most perfect mouth. Cracked, dry lips can be as unattractive as a bad complexion, so always use some sort of moisturized base to keep your mouth soft and pliant before applying your lipstick.

The only way to truly achieve a clean lip line is to utilize a lip-liner pencil, a lip brush or both. A bit of practice is in order if you wish to wield them effectively, but once you have the hang of it, you'll realize why I stress their importance. It is virtually impossible to get special professional corrective effects without them.

I have a personal problem for which I have learned to compensate, using these two valuable beauty aids. My upper lip line is too indefinite to suit me, and my mouth is not quite wide enough for my face. As a solution, I use a dark shade of lip-liner pencil to draw a false lip line slightly above the outer edges of my natural lip line, on both top and bottom. I extend the corners slightly. I make the line quite heavy in the beginning, because when I begin my blending process later, the heaviness reduces to an acceptable width. Next, I apply the lipstick or, in my case, a combination of lipsticks, with a brush. (A factor in favor of using a brush is that it's a money saver, because you can use every single dab of lipstick in the tube.) I use a lipstick that is slightly lighter than the lip-liner color and apply it immediately adjacent to the liner in the center of my lips. I then use a still lighter color, sometimes a frosted one, to make the final application of tone to the center of my lips and slightly on the inside of them. I discreetly blend these three separate colors into a smoothly indefinable profusion of color. I use a brush to do this, of course. In so doing, I have created a fuller, slightly larger, more sensual mouth. For sparkle, I gently blot my mouth and add a very thin covering of lip gloss. As you might suspect, my mouth looks infinitely more "kissable."

A good trick for lips that are too full is to use brown liner on the lower and upper lip lines, beginning on the inside of the natural line. Then reverse the procedure I have just outlined, using darker and darker shades of lipstick so that the final center color has the greatest depth and intensity.

A very lush illusion can be created when you use a light brown lip liner after you have applied your regular lipstick. Encircle your mouth, ever so lightly, slightly extending the corners in an upward direction and blending into the foundation.

I have noticed that nonmodels tend to stick to one kind of lipstick application for all occasions. It's too bad. In my estimation, that's analogous to wearing the same dress every day, day in and day out. It is so easy to find new and exciting ways of doing your mouth, why not try some? All it takes is an awareness of what's going on in makeup trends and a little spirit of adventure. You'll need a few undisturbed moments in which to practice and experiment, but when you've found a new "look," you'll be getting plenty of compliments. Won't that be nice?

Professional models who really know what they're about always make a last-minute cosmetic check. They use a modern cosmetic mirror that produces the exact lighting conditions they desire—day or night; indoor or outdoor—to avoid looking overstated or understated, as the case may be. A mirror of this sort more than pays its own way in the confidence you have when you check your own finished product.

TOUCH-UPS

A careless touch-up can ruin the most beautiful makeup. Too many women just add layer upon layer of cosmetics until they have a caked, heavy look at the end of the day. To avoid this, keep your shine toned down by blotting with a makeup blotter. If this doesn't solve the problem, start from scratch.

If your skin is very oily, you may have to do this several times a day. That doesn't mean your eye makeup has to come off too. You can wash your face carefully without disturbing your eyes and eyebrows. Use a cotton-tipped swab, dipped in gentle creamy cleanser, to freshen your undereye. When eye shadow has caked or creased, do the same above the eye. In that way you have clean skin, freshly made up, and can spare yourself the time it takes to reapply shadow, lashes, mascara and brows. Make every attempt to preserve your fresh, "alive" look.

OFFICE BEAUTY KIT

If you're a career woman, as I am, you'll find an office beauty kit just about as important as the one you have at home. You'll feel better, and work better, when your makeup is always impeccable.

Here's a list of handy supplies for your desk drawer:

Makeup-remover pads or small container of cleansing cream/lotion
Soap
Moisturizer
Foundation
Mascara
Shadow
Eye liner and brush
Blusher for cheeks
Hairbrush and comb
Hand cream
Nail file and polish for repairs
Tissues
Perfume or toilet water

POSTLUDE

The New You

The woman who wants to create her own new "look" in the way in which we create one for a model has to make a very honest appraisal of herself. She alone can decide on a self-improvement plan and make a list of what changes are in order. She alone can arrange them according to priority.

But perhaps I can help.

Let's start with attitude and motivation.

A woman who wants to be beautiful should have a consuming interest in order not to become disenchanted when she doesn't achieve immediate results in her beauty campaign. It can be a hobby; a recreational activity; a community-service organization; a career. Whatever she elects it to be, her involvement makes her more exciting, more interesting, more socially and intellectually desirable as she pursues the muse of beauty.

Whether she lives in a tiny little town or a large metropolis, a woman can always set her sights higher—get herself moving upward toward a new, more scintillating self. If she has a tendency to be lazy about reading, she can establish a program that makes her aware of the world beyond her career or special interest. I'm a serious offender in this regard. I have "tunnel vision." I get myself on a course of action and see nothing to the right or left. I know exactly what the goal is and get straight at it instead of being a bit freer and taking in some of the other pleasures of life. I'm too intense, so I have to fight against that as other women have to fight *for* it. Draw your own battle lines and concentrate on winning.

Adjusting to a whole new way of thinking and feeling is never easy, and in certain social environments it can be next to impossible. If a woman is always with the same people, where can she get inspiration and stimulus for change? I think she literally has to go out and look for it.

When it comes to physical appearance, she must weigh her pluses and minuses. A very diminutive woman can add to her charm by accentuating her petite good looks rather than trying to compensate for them with high hairdos and higher heels. The most important things, I would say, are face and hair. A super haircut should come first, then experimentation with cosmetics. Any woman who wants to look beautiful can certainly leaf through the fashion magazines and find new styles that are enticing. She can paint a face, but she has to accustom herself to the new lady she sees in the mirror. She has to let herself "grow" into her new visualization. When she gets compliments on the early changes she's effected, she will try other new things with confidence.

I firmly believe that achievement of a "New You" stems from the inner security of knowing that other people like the way you look and find you attractive.

For me there is no such a thing as a "total woman," for a woman should be stimulated to greater and greater effort, greater and greater achievement of charm and beauty.

Looking back on my nine years as a model and ten years as a models' representative, I know I've gone through several periods in which I resolved to change seriously and with purpose. I meant to look different. I wanted to be a superfine human being. I wanted it instantly, as most women do, but it just doesn't happen that way. It happens little by little over a period of time, but it is cumulative and worth the energy.

Each time, I started at the beginning. I was too heavy; my skin wasn't clear enough; I was pale; my hair wasn't glowing as it should have been; my fingernails needed to be longer; a pedicure was in order. These were physical things, to be sure, but they were manifestations of my self-neglect, and they were all within my control. I could change them if I wanted to.

To deal with them, I started with a sauna three times a week. I exercised every morning for an hour and every evening for a half hour. I took long baths in fragrant oil to freshen my skin. I gave myself some facials. I really worked on the "physical me." I had a haircut and brushed my scalp every night. I set my hair and tried a new hairstyle each day. As the days passed I looked handsomer.

Then, as so many of us do, I became the victim of my own impatience. That's dangerous, for each plateau like this tends to discourage the would-be beauty. One day, however, I could see the transformation in the mirror and feel it in the overall sense of zest for living that was returning to my body and to my mind.

My vigor was renewed. I applied myself to straightening my closets; fixing my seams, snaps, buttons and hems; shining my shoes and purses regularly. I made everything fresh for that bandbox look. It gave me a feeling of accomplishment and led me right into improvement of my brain. I read every night. I took French lessons once again. When I went out socially, instead of just sitting there and listening I tried to participate. I attempted to be more charming, more alive, to speak about the things I was reading and to learn more from others. I became stronger and more mature—mature enough to admit publicly to all the things I didn't know.

Still, I didn't feel complete. I know there are always new fields to conquer. So I've gone on a self-improvement campaign every few years of my life, and I guess I always shall. There is no "total woman" for me.

Every spring, many women resolve to make similar changes; to become more alert and contemporary in their thinking. But they lose that follow-through when fall sets in, and that tends to keep them on the brink of being beautiful rather than leading to actual achievement of their beauty goals.

The key to an ongoing "New You" therefore is to continue to care about yourself and extend that caring to the people around you. One can't expect miracles, so look for slow but steady beauty results.

I have always had a very bad temper that flares up whenever things don't go my way. I'm not saying that I have it entirely under control even today, but I do think I've sufficiently subdued this negative trait to have stopped subjugating others to my anger. It didn't happen overnight. I had to work on it, since I was unwilling to go on hurting those around me. Each person must define her own negative traits and bring them under domination.

I preferred to create a feeling of happiness in my loved ones and in myself because I do believe the more satisfied one is with oneself, the better able one is to project good looks and good feelings to others.

Sometimes we have to psych ourselves into control; maneuver ourselves, if you will. Here I go back to discipline and determination. One starts the day not just by having to, but by wanting to. There is a difference. If you work at something just to be occupied, that's one thing; but when you have a goal in mind, that already makes you a better human being because you're working toward an idea, an ideal, You're committed. You're pleased with yourself; therefore you want to go on improving.

Those who don't have a goal, or a series of goals, had better develop some important thrust for their existence, and the sooner the better.

If you sense that there are better things beyond the present, that there's more to learn, to understand, to experience, then certainly you have the power to look inside yourself, find the things that need change and change them to create The New You.

The quickest way to self-improvement is through love. A well-integrated woman wants to do everything that entices and suits her lover, her husband, her children, her associates. She is already well on the way to success in augmenting her good qualities and diminishing her negative aspects; but the circle is closed only when her desire to please reaps the reward of their reciprocated love and consideration.

I am dedicated to the principle that a woman should express herself. I'm not saying every woman has to move out into the work force to do that; but I am saying that in order for a woman to be interesting to others, she has to be interesting to herself and she has to be interested in growing with those around her.

To be The New You, lay out a master plan for your own happiness and development. There are many women who are aware they are miserable, many who know what they need to do to realize their greatest potential, yet they remain fixed in a stultifying situation. That indicates to me that they actually cherish their neurotic malaise, or they're too lazy to alter the circumstance that creates it—or too frightened to search for a new self. They don't really give a damn about themselves. I feel the only way a woman can enhance her loveliness is to live a unified but vivid existence.

Beauty is for the woman who does the most with her physical appearance; who elevates the quality of her thoughts; who keeps an open mind and an open heart; who is bright, gentle, kind and sensitive to others. She's beautiful for them, and in so being, she becomes beautiful for herself.

You're beautiful if you care about change. And I do.

The overwhelming desire for change is the beginning of The New You—and there is no end.

INDEX

219

Index

Index

Muscles
  arm, 100
  buttocks, 80, 106
  chest, 100
  proteins and, 110
  stomach, 66, 70
  see also Muscle Stretcher Exercise
Muscle Stretcher Exercise, 104–05

Nails
  beauty tips, 176–77
  false, 175–76
  mending, 175
  see also Manicure; Pedicure
New York, 10, 107
"New You"
  and inner security, 216
  key to, 217
  and love, 218
  self-development, 218
  things that need change, 218
Nutrients, beauty, 110–12
Nutrition, 11, 108, 112, 113
  see also Food; Vitamins

Paris, 10, 107, 159
Patti Nails, 176
Pedicure, 42, 177–79
Permanents, hair, 190
Physical Types, 108
  see also Body Shape; Clothes, Body-
    Shaping; Figure
Pinch test, 34–35
Pores, facial, 37
Posture, 34
Proportions, Body, 35
  Desirable Proportions Chart, 36
  see also Clothes, Body-Shaping
Protein, 110, 113, 180

Recipes: *see* Hummingbird Diet Recipes
Riboflavin: *see* Vitamin B2
Rinses, Highlight, 185
  see also Hair Color

Sauna, 216
  see also Sauna, facials
Sauna, facials, 165, 166, 167, 169, 211
Security, inner, 216
Self
  -appraisal, 215
  -development, 215–18
  -evaluation, 34–38, 108, 216
  -improvement, 215, 217, 218
  negative traits, 217
Sewing, home, 159

Shampooing: *see* Hair Care
Shape, body: *see* Body Shapes
Shashlik, 121, 128
Shaving, 37, 42, 171
Skin
  and iodine, 112
  premature aging, 166, 170, 171
  and protein, 110
  see also Skin Care; Skin Types;
    Vitamins
Skin blotches, 111
Skin Care
  basic, 165
  face pampering, 164
  night/morning, 165
  price of shortcuts, 163
  special, 165
  and vitamins, 164
  washing, 166, 167, 168, 169
  see also Manicure; Pedicure; Skin; Skin
    Types
Skin Types
  combination, 37, 164, 168–69
  dry, 37, 164, 166
  oily, 37, 164, 167, 214
Snacking, 117, 118
Solid fats, 111
Sports vs. exercise, 43–44
Spot Shaper Exercises
  abdomen, 72–73
  abdomen and legs, 74–75
  abdomen and thighs, 68–71
  bust, 96–101
  buttocks, 76–85
  hips and legs, 90–91
  hips and thighs, 86–89
  thighs and calves, 92–95
  waist, 52–55
  waist and abdomen, 64–67
  waist and hips, 60–61
  waist and legs, 56–59
  waist and thighs, 62–63
  see also Exercise
Straightening, hair, 190
Stretch exercise, 45
Style, sense of, 159, 160
Sun and skin, 170

Teeth, vitamin C and, 112
Tension, 106, 171
Thiamin: *see* Vitamin B1
Thighs, exercises for
  thighs and abdomen, 68–71
  thighs and calves, 92–95
  thighs and hips, 86–89
  thighs and waist, 62–63

223